MW01257736

Gentle

Gentle

REST MORE, STRESS LESS, and LIVE the LIFE YOU ACTUALLY WANT

Courtney Carver

balance

New York Boston

Balance
Hachette Book Group
1290 Avenue of the Americas
New York, NY 10104
GCP-Balance.com
@GCPBalance

First Edition: February 2025

Balance is an imprint of Grand Central Publishing. The Balance name and logo are registered trademarks of Hachette Book Group, Inc.

The publisher is not responsible for websites (or their content) that are not owned by the publisher.

The Hachette Speakers Bureau provides a wide range of authors for speaking events. To find out more, go to hachettespeakersbureau.com or email HachetteSpeakers@hbgusa.com.

Balance books may be purchased in bulk for business, educational, or promotional use. For information, please contact your local bookseller or the Hachette Book Group Special Markets Department at special.markets@hbgusa.com.

Interior book design by Bart Dawson.

Library of Congress Cataloging-in-Publication Data

Names: Carver, Courtney, author.
Title: Gentle : rest more, stress less, and live the life you actually want / Courtney Carver.
Description: First edition. | New York : Balance, 2025. | Includes index.
Identifiers: LCCN 2024035493 | ISBN 9781538765210 (hardcover) | ISBN 9781538765234 (ebook)
Subjects: LCSH: Self-actualization (Psychology) | Compassion. | Self-help techniques.
Classification: LCC BF637.S4 C3697 2025 | DDC 158.1—dc23/eng/20240927
LC record available at https://lccn.loc.gov/2024035493

ISBNs: 9781538765210 (hardcover), 9781538765234 (ebook)

Printed in Canada

MRQ-T

10 9 8 7 6 5 4 3 2 1

For Bailey
This is our place. We make the rules.

Contents

Introduction

The Gentle Way

Most of us have spent too much of our lives being anything but gentle with ourselves or the world around us. Treating ourselves and others gently, creating moments of softness and stillness, is so often viewed as weakness, as giving up. But the simple fact is: We are worn out. We are tired of pushing through, tired of thinking we have to overdo everything, all the while pretending that we thrive under stress (as a boss I once had loved to remind me). As a result, gentleness has become an absolute imperative. It's time to create our own rules, new rules, gentle rules.

I host a six-day challenge online, called *The Tiny Step Simplicity Challenge*, which is all about going slow and creating habits that stick with less effort and more ease. By day three, there are people in the group who are frustrated that it's taking so long and that we are doing so little each day. Yet by day six, I'm getting emails from people who are absolutely shocked about the progress they've made and how good they feel, relieved to be released from how they've always tried to change in the past. Maybe you've had the same experience. You approached something you wanted to fix, change, or do better with a "push through at any cost" mentality. But having worn yourself out, you find yourself collapsed on your couch, only to discover after a few minutes, hours, or days that what you really needed was...some rest.

If you've ever been through the vicious cycle I've described above, and especially if you are in the midst of it right now, I want to offer you some immediate relief:

You aren't broken.

You don't need to be fixed.

You are not alone.

There is a gentler way.

I get it. I'm here for you. Hi. I'm Courtney, I write books, and I'm a simplicity advocate. I write and speak and guide people who are interested in simplifying their lives for a variety of reasons. They might be interested in simplifying for physical and mental health issues, money problems, relationship struggles, busyness addictions, and sometimes all of the above. But that's not why I'm qualified or even interesting enough to ask for your attention. The reason I am here with something to offer you is this...

I have been there.

I have been sick, broke, tired, frustrated, and in a life where I struggled to figure it all out. I have been divorced, down, fired, and even diagnosed with a chronic, progressive disease. This is not me grumbling about my life; instead it's all part of my wake-up call. I'm grateful for it. In fact, I'm not sure where I'd be today without having been through all of that. I used to be a pro at ignoring what was going wrong in my life, glossing over my pain. I was a "grin and bear it" lady. Behind the scenes, I knew I was drowning. But, on the surface, the waters appeared calm.

By late 2006, I had a perfect life. At least, that was what it looked like from the outside. I had recently gotten remarried, I was working as an advertising executive for a group of luxury magazines, and my daughter was doing well in school. Looking at it from the inside, there were some problems. In addition to dealing with wild deadlines and that boss I mentioned, I was chairing an auction at my daughter's school and training for the MS 150, a cycling event to raise funds for multiple sclerosis research, because my boss had MS. Per usual, I was doing way too much. It didn't cross my mind to slow down, although it did cross my body. Always being on the go was wearing me down. I felt exhausted and I didn't see it changing any time soon. I just thought, *This is how I feel.* Then I started to experience vertigo, numbness in my face, and tingling in my hands. I had no idea what was going on but I kept feeling bad. I asked my doctor what he thought, and he said, "It's probably just an ear infection or stress from being a working mom and all." That sounded good (if a little dismissive) until a month later when I felt even worse.

That was when the tests began. My brain was scanned, my spinal cord was tapped, and I was tested in every possible way. In July 2006, while I was getting ready to ride in that event for multiple sclerosis research, I was diagnosed with multiple sclerosis. When I started feeling better (once I could stand up, close my eyes, and not fall over), I realized I would have to learn how to take care of myself. Not just what I did to get by on a day-to-day basis but *really* take care of myself. My "go big or go home" approach wasn't going to work anymore. To be honest, it never had worked but, back then, I didn't know another way was available to me. Now I knew that if I kept going like I had been, I'd probably just get sicker.

Because my propensity to overcommit and overdo was so deeply ingrained, this wasn't a spontaneous decision or an awakening that led to immediate change. At first, I tried to push through so I could prove to everyone that I was OK. Spoiler alert: I was not OK. Through every test that led to my diagnosis, I never missed a day of work. I even learned how to give myself injections and figured out what extra medicine I could take so as not to feel so sick from the medicine that was supposed to be helping my MS symptoms.

In fact, I worked harder than before. I remember once coming out of an MRI, shaking, terrified, and nauseous, and heading straight into the office thinking, *You have to keep going.* After a round of IV steroids administered at my kitchen table, I would feel terrible, but I'd still keep pushing. I would smile in the office and cry in my car. Yes, I was scared and sick, but I was a master of faking how I felt.

Are you doing this, too? Most women I know are pretty good at this. We aren't doing it to deceive or manipulate but rather to not upset others and not fall further behind in a race we already feel we are losing. Most of us never feel or think we are doing enough, giving enough, or making enough, or that who we are in the world is enough. And so, we do more. We go harder. While we hope one day it will propel us in the right direction, it inevitably makes us more exhausted, more overwhelmed, and more frustrated. And then what? We pretend harder until the day comes where we cannot show up to one more thing with a fake smile on our face. For me, that day came when I was officially diagnosed with multiple sclerosis, over the phone, at work.

So why do we always think the answer lies in doing more, proving more, having more, and pretending more? Because it's all we know. It's what is happening around us, it's the advice we've read in reputable self-help books and heard from everyone we thought was living a happy, successful life (because they kept their pain a secret, too). Someone was always trying to fix us, so we thought we were broken. And eventually, that broke us. Over the last decade and especially the last few years, what I've discovered is that our more, better, harder, faster approach to our internal exhaustion causes more damage than good.

We don't have to fix everything within us. Instead, we need more support. In addition, most of the systems currently designed to lift some of us up and hold the rest back need to be flipped on their asses. But let's start with us, with our lives, and our hearts. Instead of trying to become a better version of yourself (again), let's try something new: Trust ourselves to be kind, soft, and slow in how we treat ourselves and others, how we change our habits, and how we live our lives. Fast and furious is out. We are done fighting it and faking it. It's time to be gentle.

Gentle? you might ask. What is that? Let's start by looking at what it is not and then look at what it actually is.

Gentle *is not*...

- a sacrifice
- people pleasing
- giving up
- pretending that things are perfect
- ignoring pain in ourselves or in the world

Gentle *is*...

- the antidote to overwhelm
- an invitation to choose consistency over intensity
- easing through instead of pushing through
- creating strength in stillness
- putting yourself first
- rejecting the old rules and creating your own

Today I am symptom-free, and I haven't had a relapse or any visible progression of multiple sclerosis since 2008. My neurologist often says, "It's like your MS is in suspended animation." Yes, I have an amazing doctor and medical team and I do take conventional MS treatment *and* I radically simplified my life and removed a whole bunch of stress. I treat myself like someone I love, gently...*most* of the time. This is a practice, after all. I'm still learning, making mistakes, and continually coming back to the Gentle Me. I'm going to share what I learned in becoming the Gentle Me so you can make simple shifts to become the Gentle You. That's what this book is about—getting you back to you, the Gentle You. Becoming the Gentle You will get you further than the Stressed-Out, Overcommitted, Running-Late, Annoyed-AF-at-Everyone (especially yourself) You. Actually, the Gentle You might not get you further. She'd rather ask if you *need* to go further and remind you that you may be right where you are supposed to be, no striving or saying yes to one more thing required. More important than where the Gentle You can take you is the way this new connection to yourself will change how you feel and how you show up in the world. It's knowing that you don't have to get to the next level or climb another ladder to be in the best possible place. This is especially reassuring if you've often abandoned yourself and what you need in the name of "more." The Gentle You isn't always plotting what's next. She doesn't think of everything as a stepping stone. She doesn't have a ten-year plan. She just wants you to take a deep breath and feel good in this moment.

This book is for you if you want to...
- relax
- enjoy your life
- stop measuring yourself by what you accomplish
- reject hustle culture

- stop feeling so damn overwhelmed all the time
- say no whenever you feel like it without a big explanation
- stop pleasing others by disappointing yourself
- give up your quest to control everything
- actually show up for your life
- feel less stressed out

Good news: This is all available to you, and you don't have to work hard to get it. In fact, the way you'll get it is by working less, by easing through instead of pushing through. More than 90 percent of these changes are going to happen within you. When you decide to be the Gentle You, you won't have to make a spreadsheet about it, create reports to prove it, share it on social media, or do anything else. All you have to do is decide. Decide to be gentle. That said, it's not a one-and-done exercise. You get to decide to choose the Gentle You over and over again.

Even though I've used the phrase "be gentle" thousands of times, I still have to intentionally choose the Gentle Me. Otherwise, I default to the me who is made of everything she's ever witnessed, the me who on some level or in some cell or bone or tendon remembers every thought, word, and deed that came before. Those memories tell me what *pleases others*, what I'm *supposed to do*, and how I *should behave*, and mold me into something I am not. In that place, the cognitive dissonance shows up in the way I become paralyzed by decision fatigue or imposter syndrome. It shows up when I spin my wheels, jumping from task to task while feeling unable to focus and not taking care of myself.

When I get gentle, I remind myself that all of those thoughts, feelings, and ideas lodged in my body already happened, and most of them weren't even mine. I don't have to hold them anymore. If you wrestle with that, too, start by being gentle. If you are already thinking, *Easier said than done*, I get it! It's not easy, but is it easy now? Is the way you treat yourself today easy? If not, maybe it's OK that this new path feels easier said than done.

THE SEASONS OF GENTLE

Throughout this book, we'll unpack simple shifts and gentle practices that will help you discover why and how to be gentler without sacrificing who you are and what you want. In fact, connecting more deeply with who we are and what we want is a big part of the gentle puzzle. To get there, in this book we'll move through three seasons of Gentle: "Rest," "Less," and "Rise." Combined, these three seasons create a soft place to land as you live your life.

In the first season, "Rest," you'll consider how to pull back, relax, and reset. We'll look at why we resist rest and how we can begin to prioritize ourselves and the restful practices our bodies literally depend on to function.

The second season is called "Less." This is where you'll release the obstacles standing in the way of the life you want and the person you are. Because I've spent so much of my life focused on simplicity and letting go, I know how life-giving this season is. From decluttering your home to your calendar, releasing the excess is a critical part of becoming the Gentle You.

In the third season, "Rise," you'll learn new ways to rise up, to navigate the world, to protect your peace and move forward, not through striving and proving and working yourself to the bone but instead through stillness, sometimes silence, and always from a place of the Gentle You. In this season you'll see how to bring everything together to create and live the life you may be craving right now.

In our lives, there are times that call for slow, gentle change, and then there are the times when you just have to let that shit go. The way to tell which season of Gentle you need is by noticing how you feel and assessing your level of resistance to the changes you are making in your life. If something doesn't feel right, that doesn't mean you have to work harder. It probably just means you have to change the way you change. Changing the way you change is a core part of being gentle, and we'll return to this idea again and again in this book. When you can give yourself permission to change the way you change, you're able to drop the judgment around how you changed before.

We often punish ourselves for the way we did it before or for how we've always done it. When I say "punish," I don't mean you put yourself in time-out—taking a pause, reflecting on how you feel and how you want to move forward. (That could actually be helpful.) Instead, you punish yourself by not allowing yourself the ease, space, and grace you deserve while changing something in your life. This happens when you tell yourself, *I can't do it, I've tried before and failed*, or a million other stories that hold you back. This is true for new changes and for things you've tried to change many times before. When you want to change a habit that you've already tried to change before, you may find you often remember the last time (or the last several times) you tried to change and didn't. You remember your failure to change. You remind yourself you have no willpower or discipline or whatever it is you think you're supposed to have to be successful at making changes in your life. But there is a gentler way to change, and the seasons in this book will help you get there ... at your own pace.

THE REASON I WROTE THIS BOOK

I started writing publicly in 2010 with my blog bemorewithless .com. At the end of 2017, my first book, *Soulful Simplicity: How Living with Less Can Lead to So Much More*, was published and in 2020, my second book, *Project 333: The Minimalist Fashion Challenge That Proves Less Really Is So Much More*, came out. Both the books and the blog are very focused on simplifying your life. I write about things like decluttering, becoming debt-free, doing less, and other ways of removing stress from your life through simplicity. I don't write about simplicity for the sake of having a simple life but, rather, to help you use simplicity as a tool to reduce stress, improve relationships, and feel better. When I began this journey, I had no intention of simplifying my life. All I wanted was to be healthy. There are so many unknowns with MS. I set out to reduce as much stress as I could to live well with the condition. As it turns out, most of that stress reduction was rooted in simplicity. I realized that what I was creating for myself was not just a simpler life but the space to soften, time to pause, and awareness to become the Gentle Me.

Simplicity wasn't just the tool I used to clear out my closet. It was the path to taking better care of myself and learning what was important to me. There were some starts and stops and frustration in the very beginning; all of them came from me trying to force things, push through, and be the best, as if there is a prize for decluttering the best or for having the most organized junk drawer. Still, I had to go through those steps to learn how to make space for this more important work.

I've noticed that when starting to simplify (or starting anything we aren't sure about), we get overwhelmed with what the next steps are and rarely consider taking care of ourselves first.

Instead, we think we have to dive in and get to work. When anyone asks me how to simplify or declutter, my first line of advice is almost always, "Be gentle with yourself." People were expecting step-by-step decluttering advice or some admonishment from me to try harder, but they were carrying so much stress and hurt that I knew decluttering wasn't the first step. Being gentle was the first step. It was the natural advice I offered to everyone but myself. But the more I wrote and said those words to others, the more they settled in and worked on me, too. And the people I told passed the advice along to people they loved.

I remember the first time I heard from someone specifically about my guidance to be gentle. The email said, "Thank you. Last year I reached out to you because I was struggling to let go and you didn't push me or make me feel bad about my lack of progress. Instead, you told me to be gentle. Not only did that make it easier to let go, but now I give myself this advice and pass it on to family members when they are going through a hard time." The idea of those four words, "Be gentle with yourself," having such a beautiful impact only strengthened my belief that the way to almost everything we seek is by doing it more gently.

Now, with this book, I get to share the lessons, tiny steps, and simple shifts that worked in my life and in the lives of people I work with. I get to give you every permission slip I would have liked to give myself in the past, and finally do give myself now. I'm going to bring you some of my favorite wisdom from friends and experts, too. It's my hope that not only will reading *Gentle* inspire you to be gentler in your life but that reading or listening to this book will *feel* gentle, too. I am cheering you on and reminding you to be gentle all the way through.

A REASON TO READ THIS BOOK

You'll have your own reasons to read this book and to start being gentle with yourself, but one reason everyone can share is community. When you start to go slowly or take care of yourself in other ways, you may notice some raised eyebrows. You won't be doing things the same way as you've done them before—answering text or email messages within fifteen minutes of receipt or torturing yourself for not getting through your entire day's to-do list—or the same way other people around you may do them. That can make people uncomfortable. In the beginning, it helps to have support, to know that you aren't alone. We can be here for each other. I'll be sharing new resources at bemorewithless.com/gentle-resources, and you can always email me directly at support@bemorewithless.com.

As more of us become gentle in our own lives, it will become easier for others to be gentle, too. We can move from self-care to community care, or to including community care with our self-care. That's when our efforts go far beyond our own personal health and happiness and start to make a difference in the world. We don't all *have* to be massive world changers; collectively, our tiny steps will make a difference.

WHAT TO EXPECT

In addition to the seasons of the book I mentioned earlier, you can expect a similar rhythm or formula in each chapter. It's a gentle way of sharing information with you so you feel at home with each turn of the page. Look forward to a short story or real-world example in each chapter about me or someone else with experience, then the gentle practice mixed in with a bit of research (don't expect a bunch of math or science, that's not me). Then I'll give you a few tiny steps so you can close the gap between inspiration and action. Finally, I'll share the Gentle Step. That's the step to start with if you are low on time, energy, or motivation, just a little something to bring you in. Sometimes, that's all we need to close the gap.

At the end of every chapter, you will also be given a permission slip. In the name of prioritizing you, it's time to give yourself permission. Sometimes we withhold the most basic things from ourselves because we forget that we can just have it, do it, or take it. Give yourself permission to do anything that helps you to rise in a way that doesn't wear you out. You can re-create the permission slips or print them from the website's Gentle Resources page. Use them to reinforce what you are learning and as a not-so-subtle reminder to those around you that things are changing.

HOW TO MOVE THROUGH THIS BOOK

Obviously, I'm going to suggest you move through this book gently but—beyond that—I hope that you will move through it at whatever pace feels right to you. Think of it as the Gentle immersion program. If the concept of being gentle with yourself sounds foreign or out of reach, don't worry. If it's something new for you, it will take a little time to accept and adopt.

You may have some immediate concerns. Maybe you are wondering whether becoming gentle means you aren't strong anymore, can't have goals, or grow in your career. Does being gentle mean you can't fight for political change or stand up for yourself? Oh no. Becoming gentle means you'll get to live your life the way you want to live your life without completely exhausting yourself. It will make you stronger, more powerful, and more capable of changing the world.

Through the gentle practices in this book and being open to the idea that an effective approach doesn't have to be hard and overwhelming, you'll quickly warm to the process this book lays out. As you experiment, you'll become more confident and comfortable with the Gentle Way, and eventually you won't want to do things any other way. In most cultures, our default is usually making things harder, more complicated, and more stressful, and suffering more than necessary. Just by considering this new approach, you'll create some breathing room and reduce some of the stress you may be experiencing.

All this said, this book does have a structure and a plan, albeit a very, very bendable one. In each chapter, I will share gentle practices that will help you on your gentle journey. While I highly recommend starting in the season of "Rest," if you want to start with "Less" or "Rise," go for it. Trust yourself to know what you need right now. Choose the gentle practices that you are most curious about or the ones you think could reduce some stress in your life. When there's a practice that makes you think, *Absolutely not. No way. Never,* give it some extra attention. It's possible those are the practices you need the most. Then whenever you need a refresher or reminder, come back to any of the three seasons. Even if you decide to start all over again, give yourself the grace to do that without any shame or blame. You wouldn't expect someone you love to torture themselves with shame and blame. Put yourself in the category of "someone you love."

Pay attention to how you feel as you are reading. Are you feeling rushed or frustrated, and skimming through the book to get to the end? Those are all signals to pause and give yourself permission to read at a time that works better for you. Sometimes, if I find myself reading the same page of a book several times and it's still not sticking, I know I'm too tired, hungry, or distracted in another way to read. This happens when I write occasionally, too. Whenever I have the choice to push through or do it another time, I choose the latter. It's the gentler choice. It's not like I get more done by pushing through anyway. In those cases, I'm just going through the motions without accomplishing much. You may consider creating a routine or reading ritual to further demonstrate to yourself that this work you are doing may be the most important thing you do. However you decide to proceed, think about why becoming the Gentle You will serve you. We can figure out the *how* together, but knowing *why* you want this for yourself matters.

THE GENTLE YOU

Becoming the Gentle You is *real* self-care. It's not a quick fix. It's a meaningful practice that, over time, will soothe your nervous system and strengthen your relationships—including the most important one: the one you have with yourself. It's so hard to be kind to others when we are suffering ourselves. Yet we still dismiss our needs in the name of putting other people first, or when placing our hands on our phones before we place them on our hearts, or doing anything else that can distract us from knowing and trusting ourselves. Please don't confuse this invitation to be gentle as a request to be more pleasing to others. This isn't about being nice, smiling more, or becoming a good girl. That advice was all to benefit others. While others may benefit from you becoming gentle, it's not for them. This is for you.

Until we connect with the gentler side of ourselves, the Gentle You and the Gentle Me, we will always hear the outside voices first. The voices around us will overpower the inner voice we know (and can trust, if only we could hear it). From our families, friends, and coworkers, through the internet, self-help articles, social media, and breaking news, to the voices of our past and future. They are noisy, pushy, relentless voices that we allow in because we don't know how to listen to ourselves first, don't know we are allowed to, or don't think we deserve to.

Putting our own voice first goes against all of the messages that feel like second nature. Messages like:

Pay attention.

Listen to the experts.

Be nice.

Smile.

You can do better.

Make everyone happy.

We naturally give those messages more weight even though they have nothing to do with us, with who we are, or with the life we desire.

Our inner voice can be affected and masked by all the outside ones. It gets confusing in there when there is too much input. That inner critic—the one who says that you didn't get up early enough, you look old, nothing looks good on you, you aren't doing enough, how dare you be your age without a purpose and a passion (preferably one that pays well)—that voice is only a distillation of every negative thing you've ever heard or thought about yourself. That isn't your inner voice. It's all the other outer voices that seeped in when you were too busy, too stressed, and too overwhelmed to notice and resist them. You might have been immersed in your career or raising a family or simply trying to make ends meet. Your defenses were down. Protecting yourself from these sneaky, damaging messages requires so much energy that it's easy to disconnect from and forget your own voice and your inherent gentleness.

Peeling back the layers of your "doing" self will lead you to the Gentle You. You'll still do what you need or want to do, but the act of getting things done for the sake of getting things done will begin to lose its current attraction. Notice and question the connection between who you are and what you do. Are you making certain choices because you are trying to prove to yourself or others that you're a good, or a smart, or a hardworking person? When the things you do don't prove your worth anymore, the seduction of getting things done fades. For me, that shift arrived in two parts. First, when I knew I was sick; and second, when I noticed how much validation I craved and the way that I got it (from myself and everyone around me) from doing more things. Often, not even from doing things well or doing things I cared about, just from getting a lot of shit done. This is not a sustainable practice in feeling good about yourself. On an off day, when you get sick or your energy wanes, and you can't get the level of things done that make you feel good, you'll feel like an absolute loser.

You'd think that with general life progress and all our fancy technology, we'd be smarter about the way we get things done. When the internet and smartphones made things easier, we could have said, "Lovely, now we can get our work done in less time." Instead, we said, "Oooohhhhh great! Now we can do even more!" Today, not only are we expected to get more done, we have to do it fast *and* make it look good for social media. When I look back at my twenties—when I was raising my daughter, going through a divorce, trying to figure out my personal and professional lives—I wonder how I would have managed if I also had to photograph it all, apply a filter (because it most definitely would have needed a filter), share it, and wait for it to be judged by people I didn't know. In all seriousness, I might never have had a chance to really know myself at all.

Perhaps you feel like that now. Perhaps you feel like you don't know yourself that well, or you haven't had a chance to take good care of yourself, or you've let those outside voices confuse you or define you. It's hard to give yourself what you want and need when you don't really *know* what you want or need. Overwhelm, exhaustion, resentment, and having no idea what delights you anymore— these are a few of the signs and signals that indicate you've given yourself to everyone but you. So how do you come back to you? We are going to explore that throughout the book but, at a glance, it's not that hard to prioritize yourself. In fact, if it is hard, make it soft. Usually that means making it smaller. For instance, instead of notifying your entire family that you won't be available for them anymore, try drinking a glass of water or taking a minute to stretch. Instead of quitting your job and telling your boss to kindly eff off, turn on your favorite music and declutter your junk drawer. Those other things may happen in time. Right now, the first step in prioritizing you is a gentle step. What is a small, soft, gentle way you can give yourself to you today, right now?

THE GENTLE WAY

You may have tried before to change your habits, change your ways, and even change your whole life (probably all at once). Do we have that in common? Time after time trying the same thing didn't work, so you blamed yourself. I did that so many times. I finally (and when I say "finally," I mean after doing it the other way for decades) realized that maybe it wasn't me. Maybe it was my approach. I was so over it. I was tired of blaming myself and going through the whole guilt/self-hatred cycle. So, I didn't try again. I didn't persevere (a more digestible way of saying "push through"), again: I changed the way I change. Instead of my very disciplined, rigid, unforgiving approach, I created a gentle one. I'll tell you more but first, here's an example of the Gentle Way:

Shortly after my MS diagnosis in 2006, when I started trying to declutter, slow down, and simplify in other ways for the zillionth time, I knew that I had to change the way I changed. I wanted my efforts to last this time. I was starting to wonder how many chances I would get. The not-so-gentle me would have made a big list of everything that needed to be simplified and then put a plan into place to do it all at once in thirty days or less. For instance, I would have immediately tried to pay off my debt, get rid of my clutter, and figure out why I was always overcommitted. On the first day, I'd feel very excited about everything I was changing. I'd think, *This is the time I really do it!* I'd make a big list, shop for anything I needed to support all the changes, and set my alarm clock for an hour earlier, because obviously I would need more hours in the day for this massive change. After the first week, and certainly by day twenty-one or thirty or whenever habits are supposed to become a regular part of our lives, I'd either be sick or frustrated or bored (or all three) and go back to my old ways. I did this with everything: new fitness habits, eating changes, money mindset, and other fixes. It was always harsh and never sustainable.

Back to 2006. I took a new approach. I'd love to tell you I did it because I had learned from my mistakes, but the truth is, I was sick, tired, and didn't have the heart to try it the same way again. This time, instead of figuring out the next year of everything I needed to change, I identified one thing that was stressful. Just one. I decided to stay with that one thing, break it down into very small steps (tiny ones), and stay with it for as long as it took. No deadline, no pressure or stress, just me being curious and making a little bit of progress every day. When the one thing started to feel routine, I'd look at the next thing. It probably took me three years to get rid of my debt and clutter, and it took much longer to slow my schedule and change my career. Three years sounds like a long time until you compare that to the decades I spent attempting to make changes with no real results, just the extra stress and disappointment that came with believing I had failed again.

The Gentle Way is going to help you start experiencing more peace and ease with the changes you want to make in your life. And the changes you are making are going to start to stick with less stress, willpower, and effort on your part. Imagine what it would be like to change your habits with ease. I'm going to tell you the three steps I've used to change the way I change. And by doing them, I've been able to create a clutter-free, debt-free, and very low-stress lifestyle. I have more time for what matters to me, and I've turned my health around from exhausted, burned-out, and chronically ill to having more energy and living symptom-free with multiple sclerosis. I developed this framework for you because I saw so many people become completely sidetracked while trying to change their lives. For example, people who were decluttering and trying to get comfortable with letting go would try to make progress before they knew how to describe why they wanted to simplify in the first place. Or there were people who were ready to pare down and discover what mattered to them, but they had virtually no support system. These people trying to simplify and change their lives weren't broken, but their systems were. Here are the three steps that shifted everything for me. You can use these steps to change almost anything you want to change in your life with less heartache.

The Gentle Way 3-Step Framework

1. Get superclear about why you want to make a change. Identify why you want to make the change you are making, to create some conviction and motivation. There will probably come a time while you are working on a specific habit change and things get hard. Someone might question the changes you want to make, or you might get frustrated. Some of these changes you want to make are going to take a while, so having a compelling reason will move you through the times when your big change doesn't feel as shiny and new. Coming back to why you wanted to make this change in the first place will help you stay committed and give you permission to make the shifts you need to be invested. Your "why" isn't another way to prove yourself or explain to others why you are doing what you are doing. It's for you, for your growth and progress.

2. Break down the big transformation into slow, tiny steps. Remove the unrealistic pressure you put on yourself to change a habit or accomplish something quickly. Just because someone else you heard about did it overnight (they did not) doesn't mean you need to do it that way. Slow progress is progress, and it's the kind that sticks. After working with people using this framework for years, the most common roadblock I see is that the tiny steps we create are still too big. The solution is to make them smaller and keep making them smaller until they feel approachable. A great example of this is when I created a morning routine for myself. Old way: Wake up an hour early and do a morning routine for an hour every day. That never worked. With tiny steps, it went like this. Set alarm for 10 minutes early and practice morning routine for 5 minutes. Only 5 minutes. Usually, I didn't have time for more but even when I wanted to do it longer I didn't. I stuck with 5 minutes a day for the first week. The following week, I set my alarm for 15 minutes early and practiced for 10 minutes. On the third week (you guessed it), I set my alarm for 20 minutes early and practiced for 15 minutes. By now, my morning routine consisted of 5 minutes each of 3 activities I enjoyed at the time (writing, yoga, and meditation).

For the following few weeks, I added *one minute* to each activity each week. Slow? Yes. Effective? Also, yes. In this example, there were a few teeny-tiny steps I repeated and increased slowly. If you discover you are struggling to make progress, check on the size of your steps. Chances are, they are still too big.

Tiny steps can be defined by the size of the step, or as something that is easily reversed so you can experiment without the extra stress (*What if I change my mind? What if this is a giant mistake?*). For example, if you want to declutter your house but get overwhelmed and stuck with the decisions of what to keep, what to donate, and what to sell, skip those decisions and hide everything instead. Since you won't be seeing your stuff every day, you'll break the emotional attachment and create space for clarity. I recommend walking around a room or your entire home and putting anything that you're thinking about letting go of into a box and then taping up the box and hiding it. Don't look at it for thirty to sixty days. At the end of that time, if you don't miss anything in the box, or you don't even remember what you hid, you can release it without any stress. If you decide to go through the boxes, you'll likely notice that you feel differently about the stuff that had such a hold on you. It won't be as challenging to decide what to do with it. Again, I call this a tiny step because it's something that is easily reversed. In most cases, it will help you let go with less stress and more ease. (Note: As you connect to the Gentle You and begin to trust yourself, these decisions become easier, *and* the practice of making these decisions will help you trust yourself more.)

My daughter, Bailey, wanted to develop a reading habit, so she committed to reading one sentence a day for a year. That's a tiny step! Some days she read much more, but it was always at least a sentence. Today, she reads more than fifty books a year, hosts a book club, and is an incredible supporter of new authors. That habit and her passion for books started with one tiny step: reading a sentence a day. If she had committed to a book a week or a chapter a day, or even a page a day, it wouldn't have been tiny enough to create a habit. Headspace, a meditation app, offers guided meditations that are as short as one minute because they know that even the busiest people can set aside sixty seconds a day to meditate. If the only option was thirty minutes, fewer people would try it.

3. Create a support system around every change you make. Create a support system. Include friends and family (only if they are actually supportive!), books, podcasts, and like-hearted people you can connect with in online and in-person communities. In your support system you can also include doctors, therapists, coaches, and other professionals who support you in different ways. When I'm working on a new habit, I share the project with the people I know will be supportive and then I create a little cocoon to protect my new habit. I surround myself with books or other resources that support the change I'm making.

This three-step Gentle Way will result in lasting change. For starters, you remove stress from the change you are making by keeping it small. You can stay focused and connected to the change you want to make because you aren't trying to do everything all at once. And these tiny steps each have a ripple effect. When you complete a tiny step, you will feel more confident. You'll create momentum and inspiration for your next change. When you choose your one thing and the tiny step or steps, consider what it feels like to give yourself permission to do one thing at a time. It's probably a big shift from your usual approach and less overwhelming. The Gentle Way invites you to change the way you change, and to take care of yourself along the way.

As you consider the ideas for how to make gentle habit changes in this book, try the ones that resonate with you, one at a time.

Leave others for another time. Modify any suggestions when you think you might make something work better for you. Just because one part of a recommendation doesn't work for you doesn't mean there isn't something to learn. Allow the practices I outline in the following pages to encourage and nurture the Gentle You. Let them help you feel softer and more cared for. May they remind you that you are worthy of love and trust. May they remind you that the person you deserve love and trust from the most is you.

Are you ready to start this gentle journey? You don't have to pack a thing. You've got everything you need.

Gentle

PART I

REST

When I was five I did anything I could to avoid naptime. I wanted to play with my friends, explore the neighborhood, and live my posttoddler life. I remember once my mom gave me permission to leave my room on my own after naptime, instead of waiting for her to come and get me. Sitting on my bed, she pointed to my little alarm clock and said, "When the big hand is on the twelve and the little hand is on the two, you can come downstairs." As she left the room, I lay down and plotted my escape. I thought I was very clever when, ten minutes into my one-hour nap, I quietly moved the hands of the clock, so the big hand was on the twelve and the little hand on the two, went downstairs, and told my mom that naptime was over. I didn't fool her for a second. She pointed to the stairs, indicating that I should go finish my nap. I have carried my aversion to rest into adulthood. How about you?

In our modern-day society, we resist rest with all that we have in us. *Work hard, play hard. Sleep when you are dead. Push through. Go above and beyond. No pain, no gain.* These are the messages we receive. Inevitably, after working hard, playing hard, pushing through, and pushing sleep off till death, we get run-down and sometimes even sick. When I became sick I would try to rest. Sort of. First, I'd load myself up with cold medicine or antibiotics and get a few more things done. I'd keep this cycle up until I was dizzy and exhausted. I remember some of the offices I'd worked in, how everyone would complain when someone stayed home sick instead of coming into work, pushing through, and infecting all of us. Those were the same work environments that encouraged starting early and staying late and frowned on the employees who worked only during their scheduled hours. Slackers.

In Japan, they have a word for this. "Karoshi" can be translated to "overwork death" and it means "occupation-related sudden death." The most common causes are heart attacks and stroke due to stress and malnourishment, but they also include workers who die by suicide due to the mental stress in the workplace. According to an article on bigthink.com,[1] karoshi has resulted in hundreds of deaths in Japan in recent years. Our culture rewards hardworking ladder climbers, overwhelmed moms, anyone that goes above and beyond, really. First prize goes to those who, literally, work themselves to death. There's no prize for taking the best naps, resting regularly, or taking really good care of yourself. In fact, some would call that selfish. How dare you take care of yourself when other people need you or when you have more work to do or when the world is falling apart? Ever wonder if part of the reason it feels like the world is falling apart is because not enough of us are resting? Indeed, as worn out as we are, it's a wonder we can hold anything together.

We've been taught that rest has to be earned. You can earn it by overworking, overachieving, and overdoing it. Even though we *can* rest and understand that it would be beneficial, we still resist. We try to prove our worth by what we get done, which means

we always feel like we have to *do more*. Within this broken measuring system, our efforts will never be enough. Let's reject this
measuring system and do what writer and psychologist Nicola Jane
Hobbs suggests: "Instead of asking, 'Have I worked hard enough
to deserve rest?' ask, 'Have I rested enough to do my most loving,
meaningful work?'"[2] Imagine how that shift would change how
we treat ourselves and how we treat others. How would it affect
our creative flow, problem-solving skills, and capacity to love?

THE CASE FOR REST

When we are exhausted,
we are:
- easily distracted
- rigid
- close-minded
- anxious
- competitive
- frustrated
- uninspired

When we are well rested,
we are:
- clearheaded
- thoughtful
- happier
- present
- more collaborative
- less stressed
- creative
- curious
- gentle

When you need a reminder of how important rest is, think
about how you feel after a bad night of sleep compared to how you
feel physically, mentally, and emotionally after a restful night. For
me, when I approach something without being rested, it's like trying to do the thing underwater. It's hard to focus, get excited, or

enjoy it at all because I'm working so hard to just function. And that's just after one bad night of sleep. Matthew Walker, a sleep researcher and the author of *Why We Sleep: Unlocking the Power of Sleep and Dreams*, says, "Sleep is probably the single most effective thing that you can do to reset both your brain [and] your body's health. I don't say that flippantly against the notions of diet and exercise—both of those are fundamentally critical—but if I were to deprive you of sleep for 24 hours, deprive you of food for 24 hours, or deprive you of water or exercise for 24 hours, and then I were to map the brain and body impairment you would suffer after each one of those—hands down a lack of sleep will implode your brain and body far more significantly."[3]

If we want more joy, ease, creativity, and alertness in our lives, we need rest and actual sleep. Let's unpack this "ease and joy" component. Is it necessary? I mean, work is work, right? This isn't a sermon on how you have to love your work or find your passion. I'm definitely not going to tell you that if you love what you do you never have to work a day in your life (because I love what I do, but it is still work). I recommend that you intentionally decide how you want to feel. If you want to feel burned-out and uninspired all the time, keep doing the pushing-through thing. If you believe that some ease and joy would make your life better, perhaps rest is worth a try. (Note: If you are thinking how impossible it is to rest in your current situation, we are going to address that. There are reasons I didn't name this book *Easy*.)

Can we really show up as ourselves for our work, relationships, passions, our life when we are always depleted of rest? We bring our exhaustion everywhere like a gold medal. Think of all the ways we love to tell each other how busy we are:

"Look at me! I'm winning the rat race. I went the hardest. I sacrificed the most."

"I don't even have to tell you how tired I am, you can see it on my face (even my face is tired)!"

"If you are wondering how I keep going, I don't know! Because I'm just a small percentage of myself. I am 25 percent me and 75 percent tired fumes."

Maybe this is you. That used to be me. She wasn't gentle with herself or others. She didn't have a clear vision of what she wanted and needed in her life. She didn't know how to take care of herself. She thought that when people said, "I don't know how you do it all!" it was a compliment, and that meant she was doing it right even though it felt so wrong. She didn't know she was worth it. She didn't know how to trust and love herself. So she looked for that validation outside of herself instead of within.

Once you see and articulate how you *want* to feel compared with how you really feel, even though it may also be upsetting at first, you may find it a relief. You may wonder how you've been operating the way you have without energy. How did you push through all of that depletion? Why did you? Why was exhausting yourself on a regular basis the normal pace and expectation in your life? When I thought about this for the first time, I was outraged, until I remembered all the energy it took to be outraged. At some point, I was all out of outrage. I decided that instead of pushing through, I would just rest through.

When it comes to sacrifice, we often don't rest because we don't think we have enough—enough money, enough time, enough help, and so on and so on, the list can be endless—but we know other people are depending on us to keep going. We worry about what we'll miss, what won't get done, and how far behind we'll fall. The critical mistake here is that we don't look at what we sacrifice by not resting. It can be helpful to look at the pros and cons of resting:

What we sacrifice when we rest

- getting more things done
- outside approval

What we sacrifice when we don't rest

- getting things done well
- our overall wellness (mental and physical health)
- our relationships
- our creativity
- our impact on the whole world

See? You will sacrifice less when you rest more.

WHEN YOU MUST REST MORE

It can't be overlooked that some of us need to rest more than others. If you are a woman, if you are Black, Indigenous, or another person of color, are Trans, have a disability, are dealing with chronic illness or another disease, or are marginalized in another way, society often seems to suggest you rest even less than everyone else. You must work harder to prove yourself. For the sake of clarity, throughout the book, when I use the term "woman," I am using it as a catch-all for anyone who understands themselves to be a woman or was socialized as a woman. As a white woman with an abundance of privilege, I don't have much experience here, with the exception of having been diagnosed with multiple sclerosis. Even then, I had the privilege of being white, having medical insurance and care, and the support of my family and my employer (because he had MS, too). And yet, in spite of all this, I still did not know that rest was an option. When I got my diagnosis, even in the midst of being regular-exhausted, scared-exhausted, and sick-exhausted, I strove to keep up my unsustainable pace to show everyone that I was strong, capable, and well. My actions said, "LOOK. I'm fine. I can still do it all. Don't write me off." My heart said, "I am not fine."

You can't write a book about rest and not include and thank and praise Tricia Hersey, the author of *Rest Is Resistance*, also known as the Nap Bishop.[4] In that brilliant book she says, "The deprogramming from our brainwashing will take intention and time. Rest is a meticulous love practice, and we will be unraveling from our sleep deprivation and socialization around rest for the remainder of our days. This is a blessing. Rest is radical because it disrupts the lie that we are not doing enough. It shouts: 'No, that is a lie. I am enough. I am worthy now and always because I am here.' The Rest is Resistance movement is a connection and a path back to our true nature. We are stripped down to who we really were before the terror of capitalism and white supremacy. We are enough. We are divine. Our bodies don't belong to these toxic systems. We know better. Our Spirits know better."[5]

If you have any kind of disability or difference, you've likely been impacted by ableism. Not only might you have less energy because of the body you are in but, also, your energy is likely to be sapped as a result of being part of a marginalized community. The Center for Disability Rights explains ableism as "a set of beliefs or practices that devalue and discriminate against people with physical, intellectual, or psychiatric disabilities and often rests on the assumption that disabled people need to be 'fixed' in one form or the other."[6] And what about the experiences that aren't immediately (or at all) visible? We can't always see mental illness. We can't see many chronic illness symptoms. In the early days of MS, I remember struggling through a relapse and friends saying, "Well, you look great." I'd smile, thank God for good makeup (my internalized ableism made me petrified of coming across as disabled or ill), then I'd continue to hold on to the wall to keep my balance. Some of you may fall into more than one of these marginalized categories, meaning their impact is multiplied.

It's important to recognize that we're not all starting from the same place. When it comes to bringing more rest into your life, the quantity and/or extent of the shifts you need to make in your life may be more or less or smaller or bigger than for others reading this book. We all deserve rest. If the answer was doing more, we'd all be perfectly content. I encourage you to try the opposite and rest more, do less, and reconnect with yourself. Rest brings us back to the gentlest versions of ourselves.

WHEN YOU CAN'T REST MORE

If you just brought a baby into your home, are going through a divorce, taking care of an aging parent, have teenagers, recently started a new job, are experiencing symptoms of perimenopause or menopause, or are navigating another stage of life that is messing with your ability to rest, you may be in a temporary state of exhaustion. It may be extra challenging to rest right now. There may be a medication you take that won't allow you to rest, or maybe you drink too much coffee. Let me be clear: I'm not coming for your coffee. I'm just saying that there are so many factors to consider in becoming the Gentle You. Let this be part of your noticing and accepting when it comes to your energy levels and rest cycles. See how temporary it is. If it's a longer version of temporary, consider modified versions of being restful. This season of rest, and the practices that support it, are all about being gentle with your energy, your body, and your heart, even when it might seem more complicated.

Once you establish the habit of rest and it becomes a priority for you, you'll be able to stay connected to it even during the times that you can't give it the same amount of time and energy. We always notice how important rest is during a crisis or when it seems inaccessible. By prioritizing rest all the time, not only do you build more resilience for those future crises, you may also notice that it's not as inaccessible as you think during those harder times.

It's time to take the next step. Understanding the importance of rest on a logical level is one thing, but putting it into practice will change your life. Remember the Gentle Way as you incorporate these ideas and practices. Connect to why you want to try something new or make a change, and break it into tiny steps. In each chapter of this book I will share tiny-steps suggestions, but please create and follow some of your own! It's also important to create a support system around every change you make. You may not be completely convinced that this is possible for you. You may be wondering if this is really the right time because you are in a busy season or in a moment of crisis. Let's see what happens when we rest through instead of push through, one gentle practice at time.

ONE

Rest First

To tell you that putting rest first is hard for me is an understatement. I even had trouble making "Rest" the first season of this book. My brain really wanted it to be the last—you know, save it for after we get the other stuff done. You may feel the same way because rest is often positioned as something we deem ourselves worthy (or unworthy) of. It's the carrot or the prize after we finish doing everything else. The problem with this equation is that there is always one more thing to do. Right? Is it ever all done? As I struggled to start with "Rest," I remembered my commitment to changing the way we change, taking the Gentle Way, and prioritizing what we need most. Right now, that happens to be rest.

What if we started resting right now this second? I know that feels weird because you may be thinking, *But we haven't even finished the chapter!* I know! Let's rebel and shake things up. Make a comfy spot somewhere. Set the tone and create a restful space. Turn on soft music, or enjoy the sound of rain or sweet silence in the background. Put on your softest clothing and collect your favorite blankets and pillows, anything to create an inviting, calm, cozy environment. Set a timer for ten minutes, put this book down, and rest before you read, before you learn, before you self-help, before you take one more look at your to-do list or take care of one more thing. Seriously, stop doing one more thing. Rest comes first right now.

Oh, hi. Welcome back. How did that feel? Ten minutes may not be enough time to feel completely rested or to recover from the exhaustion you've been working with. But perhaps it was enough time to reset and come back to you, or at least to give you a taste of what it feels like to rest. If you decided not to put rest first and continued reading, check in. Was it because you feel fully rested already? Or because you have too much to do? Or maybe like me, you need to understand why putting rest first is a good idea before you try it for yourself. I understand. Part of being gentle and getting to know yourself better is being thoughtful and curious about why you do the things you do and don't do. Whatever you chose, remember that you can come back to this suggestion anytime to rest and reset for ten minutes.

When I said "the exhaustion you've been working with," that might have resonated with you. Or maybe it didn't. You might have thought, *I feel fine.* Is that because you typically prioritize rest and doing less and actually feel fine? Or because you're in a bit of denial about the baseline exhaustion you live with on a day-to-day basis? This level of exhaustion can come from everything you have going on and also from a lack of consistent rest and quality sleep. I've heard from many people who say they need only five or six hours of sleep, but science says otherwise. According to the Mayo Clinic and other health experts, adults should be getting at least seven hours of sleep per night. Sleeping less than seven hours per night on a regular basis is associated with adverse health outcomes. It's important to consider not only the time you sleep but your quality of sleep. Here's another opportunity to check in—and please, do it without judgment. You are just taking note of what's going on. (Note: There is no judgment coming from me. We are in this together because we deserve to feel good. I want the best for you, for us.)

Continue to be curious and honest about the energy levels that contribute to or detract from the way you navigate your life. The goal here isn't to work toward having more energy (yet). It's to see and be honest about what you are working with overall. As I talked about earlier, there are many factors to consider here. If you ignore where and who you are and how your energy levels affect you because you still think we all have the same twenty-four hours as Beyoncé, it will be a losing battle. It's not helpful to compare yourself to others or compare yourself to yourself. What I mean by that is: If you are trying to operate with the same time and energy you had last week, last month, or ten years ago, you'll likely fall short. Not only will you struggle, but you will feel bad that you can't do the things you want to do at the pace you want to do them. What if, instead, you accepted where you are right now and worked with what you have today?

It's important to acknowledge that when you put rest first, you'll be challenging many of your behaviors around getting things done. If you consider yourself a productive person, or you're known as a person who does it all, you may have some reservations. You may want to push back or convince yourself that this season doesn't apply to you. Or, you may know that you desperately need this, but you don't see how you can possibly take the time—maybe you are working too much or you're too busy taking care of other people, or maybe there are other seemingly "restful" things you'd prefer to do, like watch TV or scroll through social media (more on this later!).

There could also be enjoyable things that keep you from resting or getting good sleep. Perhaps you stay up late knitting or doing another craft you like because it felt restful at first but then turned into a "must get done" project. (I'll admit, I've done this with a really good book before. I start out reading one chapter before bed to get sleepy and then I don't stop. My relaxing habit turns rest into pushing through.) Maybe you devote extra time to volunteering for an organization you care about. Even good things can get in the way of a healthy amount of rest and sleep. I'm going to suggest you set them aside, or even just reduce your time on them, even if you don't want to.

A note on saying no: People often talk about how hard it is to say no to outside requests, but saying no to ourselves is usually the hardest! By all means come back to that blanket you're knitting for your friend or that novel you just can't put down...but first rest. You deserve to know how you'll feel and function with an adequate amount of rest.

DO MORE NOTHING

Another reason that you might not rest is that doing nothing feels uncomfortable. As the saying goes, we are human beings not human doings. We feel guilty and frustrated when we try to do nothing. As we attempt to relax into nothingness, our brains are in constant search for more to-dos. Instead of enjoying doing nothing, we stress about everything. But resting and doing nothing may be the most productive thing you can do for yourself. If you aren't sure, consider a few compelling reasons to do more nothing:

Creating margin makes room to better handle emergencies and surprises. Test fate and plan your day, hour by hour. Don't leave any room in between tasks, appointments, or commitments. Emergencies and surprises consider this an invitation to show up and blow up the notion that you think you run the world, that you have control of things you don't control. Instead, create margin and leave a little room for nothing. The nothing may turn into something, and you'll have time for it. If the nothing is nothing, consider it bonus time for a nap, a walk, or just sitting quietly.

Adopt the habit of creating margin on your calendar, in your to-do list, and wherever you need more space in your life. Margin is an aspect of our lives that is often overlooked. In terms of efficiency, you may think you'll get less done. Maybe that's what it looks like if you are measuring over the course of a day or a week. Change your time perception and look at it over the course of a year or a decade, and chances are you'll have accomplished more (but remember, getting more done is not the point).

Less rushing around makes you a kinder person. Rushing and busyness can feel like an addiction. It's the most praised and socially accepted form of numbing out. Compare how you feel coming home after a day of back-to-back meetings with how you feel after coming home from a long walk (or a gentle stroll). You are likely to have more compassion for others when you are doing more nothing.

Time for nothing invites you to remember yourself. Doing nothing gives you the opportunity to listen to your heart and process ideas and emotions. Schedule more nothing, if only to give yourself a minute to remember who you are, what you want, and how you want to live.

The Tiny Steps

These tiny steps will help you begin to adopt the habit of resting first. You don't have to do them every day, nor do you have to do all of them. To start with, choose only one. Give one tiny step your attention without thinking about the others. Let the rest go for now—you know what happens when you try to do too many things at the same time. You can always come back and layer them in. Taking a tiny step and focusing on one thing at a time will allow you to engage, practice, and celebrate small progress.

- ❖ *Schedule rest first.* Find a five- to ten-minute block on your calendar and schedule your rest. If you have the time, schedule your rest first block every day. If you don't have the time, start by scheduling one session every other day, or even just every Sunday. If five or ten minutes isn't small enough, make it two minutes. Even though two minutes of rest may not feel like enough, it will help you establish the habit of resting, just like Bailey established her reading habit by reading only one sentence a day. If you find yourself with extra time, you could pull together the resting props (pillow, blanket, etc.) I mentioned at the beginning of the chapter. If that's not an option, just keep it simple: Sit or lie down during your scheduled rest time without extra props and prep. Make this tiny step easy. Remove all resistance.

- ❖ *Make a "Do Not Disturb. I'm Resting" sign.* Your sign doesn't need to be fancy, but if you want to add glitter, be my guest. When you want to enjoy this gentle practice of rest first, hang the sign on your door or nearby. Letting people know you are resting isn't selfish, it's kind. As Brené Brown says, "Clear is kind. Unclear is unkind."[1] Don't expect people to understand what you are doing if you don't tell them what you are doing. If you are alone with little kids and they don't understand "Do Not Disturb," see if there is a safe way to distract and entertain them so you might have a little rest. As a single mom for many years, all I can think right now is, *Thank you, Elmo.*

✢ *Create a rest box or drawer.* Keep your eye mask, noise cancellers, lip balm, and anything else that helps you rest in your kit. This is your rest care package, so don't be afraid to make it personal. Your kit could live in a tote bag, a shoebox, or a drawer. The container isn't as important as making your rest items easily accessible to keep reducing friction. If you have to spend ten minutes looking for your eye mask before you lie down, you may not have as much time to rest. To make this step even tinier, add only one item a day to your kit until you're happy with it.

✢ *Start small, grow slowly.* Go back to the first tiny step and add one minute a week to your afternoon rest. One minute a week sounds painfully slow, but it works. It was how I created my morning routine and other habits that have lasted for many years. Celebrate your patience as you slowly come back to knowing yourself, trusting yourself, and being the Gentle You.

One Gentle Step

If those tiny steps felt overwhelming, if even carving out time to read this book is a lot right now, consider one gentle step. Sit down, close your eyes, and take a few deep breaths.

Permission Slip:

I will rest first so I will be able to do my most meaningful work.

TWO

Little Saturday

After a few years together, my husband and I fell into a rut. On weeknights, instead of doing something fun, we'd eat dinner, crash on the couch, and watch a show. We both tend to wake up early, so after a full day we'd be tired, looking forward to relaxing and being intentionally unproductive. Because we were on autopilot, we found ourselves watching shows we weren't even that into. It was just time to zone out, like scrolling Instagram when you don't have the brainpower for anything else.

After a few months of this, I was feeling tired, frustrated, and disconnected. Something had to change. While we weren't interested in going out every single week—who has the energy to go out regularly on a school night?—we did want to create one night a week that was different, and more fun to look forward to. So, instead of planning a dinner out or going to an event, we each made a list of our ten favorite movies (of all time). Then, every Wednesday evening we ordered takeout (usually sushi) and then took a walk through our neighborhood. We'd come home just before the food arrived, set up everything, then watch a favorite movie from one of our lists (we'd alternate between them) while enjoying dinner. This became a fun treat we looked forward to each week.

In the Nordic tradition, Wednesdays are called Lillördag, which means "Little Saturday." They're regarded as opportunities for mini weekend-like activities. While celebrating Lillördag isn't an exact science, it helps to break up the workweek and is a reminder that we don't have to wait for the weekend or a vacation to enjoy ourselves. We often celebrate our Little Saturday with sushi and a great movie. You could celebrate Lillördag in any number of different ways, but in every case, it's an opportunity to decompress before the weekend. Perhaps Mondays won't be so Monday-ish if we know a celebration is coming on Wednesday. Could Little Saturdays put an end to the Sunday Scaries?

Embracing the idea of a Little Saturday opens the door to see how other rituals may serve you. Here are some more ideas. They may not all be a fit for you (and you certainly don't have to do them all at once), but think about whether any will help you be more rested, more at peace, and more connected to the Gentle You.

The Slowness Ritual: Leo Babauta, founder of Zen Habits and the Fearless Living Academy, practices a slowdown ritual with tea. He explains, "I find tea to be perfect for helping me to slow down, to return to the natural rhythm of life. So, in the afternoon, when things become rushed, I pause. I put some loose, whole-leaf tea (a sencha or an oolong) into a small teapot as the water heats up… I pour just a teacupfull of water into the pot, and pay attention to my breath as the tea steeps for about 30 seconds… The moment is entirely floating in this whisper of a broth, slowed by the hesitation of my attention as it stops its monkeying around and starts to enjoy the stillness."[1]

If tea isn't something you enjoy, try this slowdown ritual with any beverage or snack. Maybe you could mindfully build a delicious plate full of your favorite treats. Pro tip: Before you dismiss any of the suggestions in this book (or suggestions in general) because they don't make sense in your life, or they feel out of reach or unrelatable, shift them so they do work for you. That is a gentle practice in itself.

Maker Sessions: Creating art for the sake of creating art reminds us that not everything has to be productive, shared on social media, or judged in any way. Even if you have no skill, writing, dancing, painting, baking, or another way of making something out of nothing is a relaxing ritual that removes you from your daily pursuit of getting things done. We are all creative even though we don't all exercise those muscles. Do it for fun. Do it to rest. Do it to remind yourself what it feels like to do something just for you.

Bare Minimum Monday: Bare Minimum Monday is a trend started on TikTok by content creator Marisa Jo Mayes.[2] She coined the term *Bare Minimum Monday* to describe how she changed her Mondays from an overwhelming hustle-culture-pressured day to one where she does the bare minimum. Instead of working from a long to-do list, she focuses on doing only the most necessary work tasks. From there she moves on to taking care of herself, cleaning, or sometimes more work, but only if that's something she actually wants to do. You could have a Bare Minimum day on any day of the week.

Heart Practice: The simple practice of putting our hands on our heart invites us to come back to ourselves, reconnect, ask questions, and learn to trust ourselves. Choose an activity that will help you slow down and come to center—perhaps write in a journal for a few minutes about your morning, or lie on your sofa, stare up at the ceiling, and allow whatever thoughts you may have to rise to the surface. Next, put one hand on your heart and cover it with your other hand, as if you are holding your heart. It's a gesture to tell your heart, "I've got you. I trust you. I am here to listen to you." And then sit with your eyes gently looking down or closed and...

wait. The more you practice, and the safer your heart feels, the more she will speak to you. When I first started to do this practice, it felt a little weird, a little woo, but now it serves as a place to settle, rest, or reset. With a simple hand to my heart, or even when I visualize putting my hands on my heart, I can breathe easier, slow my heart rate, and get clarity when I'm feeling scattered.

Gentle January: You can make any month gentle, but the alliteration of a Gentle January, Gentle June, or Gentle July is irresistible to me. Still, don't limit yourself. Every month deserves the question, "How might I move through this one more gently?" Making January gentle might be the most challenging because there are so many expectations around setting resolutions, "new year, new you," and other things that encourage us to buckle down, get organized, and do better. We are hardwired to embrace the January hustle—but instead of trying to untangle yourself from it, experiment with the ritual of a Gentle January to reject those ideas completely. If you enjoy your new approach, it can be something you look forward to at the beginning of each year.

My first introduction to a Gentle January was an imperfect post on Instagram (those really stand out with everything else so beautifully curated). The picture that caught my attention was an image of a cozy living room corner with a pizza box, paper plates, and bottle of sriracha on a small table. The caption said, "Papa John's & paper plates. Gentle January made me do it." The creator, Karlee Flores, continued, "Today I slept in, drank my morning coffee on the couch, worked 3 hours and then promptly took some time to read next to Kiwi. I folded laundry, I put on makeup, changed from daytime cozies to nighttime jammies, drank ice water and snacked on fresh raspberries. I also didn't feel guilty about any of it. I didn't feel like I failed something. I didn't need to deserve today. I took it for myself. And, it felt great."[3] I deeply connected to her mention of not feeling guilty. We'll talk more about the way we hold guilt in a bit. We love to feel bad for doing things that feel good.

While not all of us can get away with working for only three hours in a day, we *can* all create a Little Saturday or a Gentle January for more joy, rest, and resilience and to shift closer to a gentler way of being. For the sake of becoming the Gentle Us, these rituals are an invitation to ease in. They are a special place to start. Becoming the Gentle You may start with a Gentle January or even a Gentle March. I'd start with whatever month you are in right now. If there isn't room to make this list or create a Gentle January or Little Saturday, is there something you can remove? Is there another habit or practice that isn't serving you right now? What's on your plate? What can you remove, even if it means having a difficult conversation or feeling uncomfortable about changing your mind? For example, could you let the school know that you can't bake brownies for the bake sale this time, or pass on a dinner invitation? You do get to change your mind, chart a new path, and even back out of commitments and obligations. These shifts may be temporary as you make a little room for you. We'll talk more about getting rid of things that remove you from your life in the second season of this book.

The Tiny Steps

These tiny steps will help create your own Little Saturday or another ritual to look forward to midweek (or anytime), instead of saving all the goodness for the weekend.

- ⁒ *Pick one ritual.* Even if they all sound lovely, choose one from the list above. If it's something you can start right away, tiny-step your way into it. If you need more time or planning, brainstorm your ritual and put it on your calendar.

⚡ *Invite a friend.* If one of these rituals would be more fun with company, invite a friend to join you. You can frame it as a minichallenge, each sharing your own approach and then trading notes as you move through your rituals.

⚡ *Create your own ritual.* Perhaps your vision of a restful ritual doesn't match the ones in this chapter. Maybe you want your ritual to be a silent walk, yoga nidra, or something else. You may even want to create a combination or fusion of some of the rituals shared in this chapter. As always, do what's best for you. It's how you'll learn to trust yourself.

One Gentle Step

If those tiny steps feel like way too much, or you can't figure out where to start, take one gentle step. Instead of committing a full evening, choose a way you'd like to experience a Little Saturday for an hour or so. For instance, instead of watching TV after dinner, try a game or puzzle. This eliminates planning, overthinking, and committing to something you aren't sure about yet.

Permission Slip:

I will not feel bad for doing things just because they make me feel good.

THREE

The Circle

It's December 2018, I'm sitting in a conference room with about two hundred other women, and I'm anxious. It's partly because, as I have an introverted nature, a room full of people will do that to me. It's also partly because I have to give a speech myself that afternoon. But mostly, it's because of who's on stage: Elizabeth Gilbert, aka the woman who has shifted the way I think about my life, time and time again. And now, she's doing it again. She's speaking about the revolution of the relaxed woman. She says that to be born a woman is to be born anxious. She explains that this is because we always have had to worry about our safety, the safety of our families, and even of people we've never met before all over the world who are living in unstable environments (think climate change, divisive politics, etc.). She goes on to share that if you google the term "relaxed woman" you'll (problematically) find images of slim, rich, white women getting massages and spa treatments. She says she has been in the homes of many women, who appear successful. They seem to have it all and they are literally dying of anxiety. So, if you think once you have made it you will be relaxed—think again. We are taught to keep our defenses up, and that is not relaxing.

DRAW A CIRCLE

Chances are that you have too much on your plate right now. That may include impossible deadlines, your child's activities, medical appointments, texts to return, people to stay in touch with, disturbing news headlines, relationship tension, money stress, social media, home improvements, and the other regular things we manage daily. Too. Many. Things. Throw in a holiday, a surprise visit from a family member, or worse, trauma, tragedy, or grief, and nothing is manageable anymore. If you make a list of everything you have going on, you may notice that you are only one unexpected thing away from a total breakdown. There's no margin of error. You want to relax, but even the idea of taking your hands off the wheel is debilitating. You feel like you must keep the wheels turning to keep it all going.

The antidote? In her speech Elizabeth Gilbert reintroduced me to Joseph Campbell, who spent his entire life studying religions from around the world. She said that once he was asked, "What is the definition of sacred?" and "How do human beings make something sacred?" He responded, "It's the simplest thing in the entire world, and you do not need a priest for it, anybody can do it. Here's how humans make something sacred: You draw a circle around it and you say everything inside this circle is holy. It's sacred because you said so." Gilbert posed the question: "If tomorrow, you still had your problems (bankruptcy, divorce, illness) but you were able to walk into a room at ease and relaxed, would you handle it better?" And I'll add a question to that: If you were more at ease and relaxed, would you be better equipped to create and live the life you desire?

If you think that it's selfish to care about fewer things, consider intention versus impact. By caring about everything, we have tremendous intentions. We worry about it all and, if we have any strength left, attempt to do something about everything. Intention is nice, but it is impact that makes a difference. We can have a greater impact on our personal health, the happiness of our families and communities, and moving the needle on projects and passions we care about when we simply do less.

Sometimes, the way we draw that holy circle around ourselves is by turning off our phones. We turn down the volume on outside expectations and turn up the volume on where our hearts are leading us. When I ask you what you care about and you give me a list of fifty things, I know that means you want to care about fifty things, but instead you care about nothing. When everything matters, nothing does. When you start caring about only the things you want to care about and not the fifty (or more) things you believe you are *supposed* to care about, that's power.

Relaxing is a practice. Becoming a relaxed woman is a process that involves some back-and-forth, some slips and slides. Even though I live with less, do less, and care about less in so many ways, I still get overwhelmed. I lose sight of what matters. I watch too much news or worry about something that is completely out of my control. I forget that it's not my job to answer every single email in my inbox. When I notice that I am overwhelmed, I reset, make an afternoon tonic, and come back to myself and to what "enough" means to me. I draw a circle around myself and I stand in it.

The Tiny Steps

These tiny steps will help you direct your energy to what you care most about instead of trying to care about everything.

- ⁖ *Draw your circle on paper.* Write down the most important things on the inside of your circle. List everything else outside of the circle fighting to get inside. Question the things inside. Why do they deserve your attention? Notice how sometimes even the things you like or are interested in might need to shift outside your circle for now because there just isn't enough room for everything inside. As new things come up, add them to the outside of the circle. When there is room, you can bring them in. Otherwise, it's a no, or a "not now."

❧ *If a circle doesn't work for you, make lists.* The first list will include what you care about most. This should not be a long list. The second list will include the day-to-day things that must get your attention. The third list are things you'd like to care about but know you don't have room for right now.

❧ *Make a lovely, bright, calming afternoon tonic.* Let the whole process be restful and renewing. Turn your phone off and give each part your full attention. When you cut the orange, can you see the zest in the air? When you squeeze the lemon, can you smell the citrus? As you boil the cinnamon sticks, can you see the spicy steam rise from the pot? And then, when you sit to sip (without doing other things), what do you taste? Once you finish, and rinse and dry your cup, check in. How did this practice in rest and presence work for you? At the end of this chapter is my recipe if you want to give it a try.

One Gentle Step

Not up for the tiny steps today? That's OK! Skip them for now and take this one gentle step. Simply identify one thing you'd put in your circle. Just one.

Citrus Tonic Ingredients

4 cups hot water   7 cloves   1 lemon

1 orange (sliced)   1 teaspoon chopped   1 teaspoon honey

2 cinnamon sticks   ginger

Add water, sliced orange, cinnamon sticks, cloves, and ginger to pot and boil for 5 minutes. Squeeze lemon and add honey to your cup. Pour strained water into cup (there will be extra so you can share or enjoy a second cup).

Are there any magical healing properties in this cup of tea? Maybe. I don't know or care, really. The magic here is the time you are devoting to something you care about: you.

Permission Slip:

It's OK if I just care about the things that matter most and stop trying to care about everything.

FOUR

Underreact

"Mom, stop yelling."

"I'm yelling?"

"Well, it's your kind of yelling."

As my daughter was growing up, we had this conversation more than once, and it usually ended in laughter because I wasn't yelling at all. Instead, I'd paused and gotten quiet. I'd responded softly. That was me yelling. It's rare that you'll get a gasp out of me, let alone a yell. I just can't work myself up into that kind of response anymore. There are some exceptions, like when I'm very surprised—for instance, the time I walked quickly around our kitchen island and the corner of the countertop caught my hip. I didn't see it coming, it hurt like hell, and I did not whisper the obscenities that flew out of my mouth. From time to time, I might raise my voice in a heated conversation, but it's rare. Usually, I want to take my time, protect my nervous system, and consider a gentler approach.

I no longer like adding drama to a potentially stressful situation. I don't want that drama for the situation, or for my insides. I used to overreact, but it never seemed to help. Instead, it always made things worse because it brought about more drama, stress, confusion, and chaos. It also hurt me. And it definitely wore me out. Overreacting felt like experiencing the same thing twice: once when it happened, and again when I brought all my outrage to the situation. My heart felt double the weight of any circumstance. Now, if I momentarily get caught up, feel outraged, and begin to overreact, then as soon as I notice what's going on, I pause and come back to myself. I remember that I don't want to spend time or energy being outraged, especially the kind that encourages me to commiserate with other outraged people and dive deeper into our collective rage. It wears us out to the point where we can't take effective action at all. To be clear, I'm not saying there isn't plenty to be outraged about in the world. I'm saying that overreacting is not where our power lies. Pausing creates a gap between feeling upset and acting out, enabling a calm, focused response.

Whether it's a world event, a business situation, or something more personal, when we overreact our desire to quickly find a solution leads us to rush and make assumptions about what's going on. It also usually includes extra stress for everyone involved. Before you know it, all parties begin to react to the extra stress instead of to the actual situation. The art of underreacting is to move from outrage to making a real difference while still taking care of ourselves.

If you are the kind of person who overreacts and rushes in, I get it. You might think you can bypass the pain of what you are experiencing by getting superproactive and taking control. What's more likely is that the rush of overreaction usually leads to more pain, not only for you, but for everyone around you. What would happen if you waited instead? I've seen so many problems in my life resolve on their own without my having to insert myself. One of the benefits of not checking email frequently is that I'll see one email asking for my help in finding or fixing something and then a second email from the same person saying they found or fixed the thing they were asking about. I know there are exceptions—like putting out actual fires, for instance, but even emergency personnel are more effective when they are calm.

Let's look at some practical ways making this shift from losing your shit to calmly taking action can be beneficial in your life. When you aren't constantly losing yourself in overreaction and overwhelm (they often go hand in hand), you will smile more. You'll create more space for focused work with less distraction. I'm not a doctor, but I think it's safe to assume that barring a unique medical issue, when you underreact, your heart rate and blood pressure will be lower, you may experience less anxiety, and you'll feel calmer. This will lead to a healthier, calmer you and give you space to connect again to the Gentle You, because she is easier to trust than the overwhelmed, outraged you.

Melissa Urban, author of *The Book of Boundaries*,[1] suggests that boundaries can help you better navigate situations where you might tend to overreact. In an Instagram reel, she shared some specific action steps to help. First, she recommends having a few generic phrases that you can employ, like, "Oh, that doesn't feel good." Or "That is not a conversation I want to have." Next, she says to have a few conversation topics that you are willing to talk about, like "your sister's new dog or your aunt's vacation." And finally, Urban says, "Have your exit strategy ready. Go for a walk, go make a phone call or leave early."[2]

UNDERREACT ON THE INSIDE, TOO

Often the depth of our inner reactions to difficult or challenging moments—like the bottom of a massive iceberg—never see the light of day. Imagine a time when you've had a heated discussion with someone and, long after it ends, you are still replaying it in your mind over and over again. You are hard at work inside your head, thinking all your thoughts, having a full-on pretend conversation with that person. "I should have said this instead of that." Or "If we talk again, and she says this, I'll say this." Or "I would never have done that," or whatever other road you go down. All this life energy you are spending is based on assumption, on something that hasn't happened yet, or on things that may never happen. This is classic inner overreacting. It's nice that no one else has to suffer through this endless ruminating, but what are you doing to yourself? We've all done it. Right? I'm not the only one? How do we stop the inner spinouts?

Note (I've already mentioned this but it's important to remember)**:** None of these practices are meant to mold you into someone who is more pleasing for others. This is for you, for *your* heart, for *your* life. It is of no interest to me if other people are happy with the way you react to something or not. But it is of interest to me if you are happy with it.

To shift the way you react (on the inside or the outside), it's less about figuring out what to do in the moment. We can't expect a big change from ourselves while we are under pressure. Instead, having daily practices and little strategies in place will help us to underreact.

What's worked best for me:

1. Daily meditation and mindfulness. One of the best results is that I've learned how to gently let go of my thoughts because I do it repeatedly while meditating. When a thought comes in, I decide if I'm going to take hold of it and beat it into submission or just let it go. I've been able to take that into my

day-to-day thoughts, too. There are other mindfulness practices that don't involve meditation but can be just as helpful, like mindful breathing, or going for a walk during which you take in every sensory detail you can. You don't have to meditate to be mindful and practice underreacting.

2. Ask yourself, "Do I care about this?" Remember the last chapter, where I discussed caring about too many things? Ask yourself the question and if you don't care, don't bother with it. You can get your mind involved in just about anything, but if you notice the thought and decide you simply don't care, it's easier to let it slip away. If you aren't sure, ask, "Why should I care about this?" or "Do I actually have the space and time to care about this?"

3. Distract yourself. If you can't let it go and you keep ruminating, get on to something else. Listen to a podcast about a very unrelated topic, do a crossword puzzle, bake something, or learn how to tap-dance. Do anything that moves you from overthinking to underreacting.

The art of underreacting does not require you to dismiss the way you feel about something. It invites you to thoughtfully consider how you turn those feelings into action. In other words, allow the feeling and make space to curate the reaction.

The Tiny Steps

These tiny steps will help you practice underreacting and put you in a headspace to feel less reactive overall.

÷. *Notice what else is going on when you typically overreact.* Do you overreact out of habit or because you are one of the following:

- hungry
- hurt
- tired
- drunk
- overwhelmed
- sick
- worried

Those things are going to lower your ability to under-react. Take care of yourself so you experience those things less or not at all. I have a rule (when I have the choice) not to engage in difficult conversations or situations where I may overreact because I am hungry, tired, or stressed. As the saying goes, please forgive me for the things I said when I was hungry. Knowing how these factors affect me, I have more grace and compassion for people who say silly things because I know they might just need a sandwich. That said, I won't be mistreated because they can't self-regulate. Neither should you.

❖ *Write about it.* This is why I journal. I'm not trying to capture memories, but instead I want to move the thoughts spinning around inside of me onto a sheet of paper where they can sit quietly. Seeing my fears and insecurities and private rages on paper defuses them and makes them easier to let go of. I can more clearly see what needs my attention and what is not worth fighting today or any day.

❖ *Walk first.* When you can't decide how you want to react, or when you think someone needs a piece of your mind, promise yourself to take a walk first. If taking a walk isn't accessible to you, think about other ways of moving your body, not to work out in a fitness way but to move around and work out the things you are unsure about. Be like Taylor Swift and "shake it off."

One Gentle Step

If it's not time to take a tiny step, consider one gentle step. Practice pausing. A five-minute pause can be the difference between you overreacting and underreacting. Take a time-out by simply waiting to respond or by saying, "I need time to think about this, let's pause the conversation/debate/meeting." This is especially helpful if something comes up and you feel flooded with emotions. It's OK to take a little time.

Permission Slip:

Things can be calm within me even when they are chaotic around me.

FIVE

Be Green-Adjacent

Before the pandemic, I could not keep a plant alive. I had zero green thumbs and had never had much success in taking care of these beautiful creatures. Today there are plants in every room of my house. I've even named some of them; I have a beautiful schefflera named Mary Tyler Moore. I knew that long walks in my neighborhood and hiking through the trees in the mountains boosted my mental health, so I thought it might be beneficial to be green-adjacent more often. Plants and trees help me feel more restful. They also remind me of this Ralph Waldo Emerson quote: "Adopt the pace of nature. Her secret is patience."

I started with one small plant that was supposed to be easy to take care of. I followed simple directions and soon realized what had gone wrong with my plant care in the past. I was giving plants too much care. They need a little sun, a little water, and perhaps a few kind words; I was so worried I'd kill them, I gave them too much attention. What they really wanted was to be left alone. Eliza Blank is the founder and CEO of The Sill, a plant store founded on this simple premise: Plants make us happier, healthier humans. She recently confirmed my realization when she was a guest on the *Soul & Wit* podcast[1] I host with my daughter, Bailey. I asked her, "What's the easiest plant to take care of for beginner plant parents?" She said that "the number one most indestructible plant is the ZZ plant, but it's important not to overcare for it. If you water it every day or take too much care, you'll kill it." Overwatering is the way most of us kill our plants. They really want to be left alone. As an introvert, I understand. Especially when I'm not feeling well and people want to take care of me, what I really want is to rest and be by myself. Now I give my plants the space they need. I let them clean the air and they ground me and cheer me up. I give them the water and care they need but not too much.

According to The Sill[2], indoor plants don't just look good—they can make us feel good, too. Studies have shown indoor plants can...

- boost moods, productivity, concentration, and creativity
- reduce stress and fatigue
- clean indoor air by absorbing toxins, increasing humidity, and producing oxygen
- add life to sterile spaces, offer privacy, and reduce noise levels
- be therapeutic to care for

A 2022 *Washington Post* article looked at several studies in an article titled, "What Science Tells Us About the Mood-Boosting Effects of Indoor Plants."[3] It cited research suggesting that houseplants can have an impact on our physical and psychological health. In one experiment, participants who spent even five to ten minutes in a room with a few houseplants felt happier and more satisfied than those in a room without plants (this is certainly my experience).

Outdoor plants and trees inspired my indoor greenery. When I want to slow my mind, let go of a long day, or seek more joy in my life, I step into the forest. Getting my feet on the trail and letting the green of the trees and warmth of the sunlight wash over me works every time. I always come off more rested than when I stepped on. In Japan, they have a phrase, "Shinrin-yoku." It means "forest bathing" or "absorbing the forest atmosphere." From an actual walk in the woods to taking care of a plant, nature helps us to rest. If you can't easily escape into the forest or climb a mountain, go to a local park or somewhere there are trees. Create the forest atmosphere indoors by adding plants to your living space.

A study done in 2021 asked the question: Does greenery experienced indoors and outdoors provide an escape and support mental health during the COVID-19 quarantine? Participants who had indoor plants experienced significantly fewer symptoms of depression and anxiety than those who did not. Another study a few years earlier showed that plants can benefit workspaces, too.[4] People who worked in offices with plants had increased well-being and fewer sick days.

The science is compelling, but try it for yourself. Notice how you feel when you are around plants and trees. Do you feel calmer and more at ease? Do plants lift your spirits? Check out your camera roll. Have you taken any pictures of beautiful plants, flowers, or other natural beauty lately? While actual plants are best, even photographs of plants can make you feel better. I follow @plantmepaul on Instagram, and watching videos of him taking care of his plants is a quick mood booster. He will make you smile.

The Tiny Steps

Even if you don't live near a forest, there are other ways to be green-adjacent. These tiny steps will help you experience the benefits of being around trees and plants.

❖ *Go for a walk in the park.* Surround yourself with the forest you have. Look for nearby parks, community gardens, or anywhere with green or trees. If it's too cold to be outside, visit an indoor botanical garden or roam around a greenhouse or plant nursery.

❖ *Take care of a plant.* I've heard that if there is a plant in sight, it can change your view and decrease your anger. Start with a plant that doesn't need a lot of your attention, like a ZZ plant. If you have pets or small children, search for plants that are nontoxic to them. In the name of tiny steps, start with one plant. After you're comfortable taking care of it, add another.

❖ *Walk mindfully wherever you are.* When you're walking, there are always opportunities to be more mindful. Give your attention to your surroundings. One walking meditation I really enjoy is to notice something beautiful and say to myself, "This is love." Interestingly, the more love I notice, the more love I notice. You may want to make this more formal and fun by playing Walking Bingo. Create a bingo card or a list of things you'd like to notice on your walk, like purple flowers, birds, bugs, and so on.

❖ *Write about forest bathing.* If pictures of plants can boost our moods, why not write about them, too? Even though I'm not surrounded by trees and I'm tapping away on my keyboard right now, I can still feel the good vibes of forest bathing. Just by turning my attention to remembering how the dirt and leaves crunch under my hiking shoes (how I love that crunchy sound!), the way the sun streams through the trees, and the noise of the aspen leaves clickety-clacking in the wind before they fall to the ground, I am transported. Write about how you feel when you are in nature. If you don't enjoy writing, try drawing a tree or a plant, or head out to add some plants to your camera roll.

One Gentle Step

If you'd rather do something even tinier and easier, try this gentle step. Sit down, close your eyes, and imagine that you are beneath a big, beautiful willow tree. What do you see, smell, feel?

Permission Slip:

I can surround myself with nature in many ways, anytime I want, and feel a little better.

SIX

Break Up with Breaking News

In April 2013, I became glued to network news. The Boston Marathon bombings had just happened and from the moment the news broke, I followed. I watched as every detail unfolded. When I had to leave the house, I'd listen in my car. I felt so scared and sick—I couldn't stop. It was a real-time, true crime spiral. I didn't sleep well that night. According to journalist Michael Easter, my nonstop news consumption of the bombing was not good news for me or others who binged the horrific event. In his book *Scarcity Brain*[1] he says, "Immediately after the 2013 Boston Marathon bombings, researchers from the University of California, Irvine, investigated two groups. The first group was made up of people who watched six or more hours of televised bombing coverage. The second group was people who actually ran in the 2013 Boston Marathon. The finding: The first group, the bombing news bingers, were more likely to develop PTSD and other mental issues. That's worth restating: people who binge-watched bombing news on TV from the comfort of home had more psychological trauma than people who were actually bombed."

Even though I was across the country and didn't know anyone involved, I absorbed the traumatic events as if they were my own. I was as far away from gentle as you could be. Eventually, I realized that giving this story my attention didn't change anything about what happened. I could have heard about what happened after the fact or read a short article and made a donation to the victims or helped in another way instead of turning my life upside down. With this understanding, I changed the way I consumed news.

Years later, I was confident that I could help Cally when she wanted to stop watching the morning news. A member of my online group the Simplicity Space, Cally was a daily watcher of a national morning TV show, and in between chefs preparing healthy recipes and fun fashion snippets, she got an unhealthy dose of national and local news. Because of the lighter, fluffier segments, she convinced herself that it was a fun way to start the day. She thought it wasn't like watching breaking news or even nightly news. Unfortunately, this nice, easy way to start the day left her feeling stressed and anxious. On top of this, she struggled to stop watching because the show was actually full of addictive breaking news. Before she was ready to make a change, we chatted about it several times. I had shared some practical strategies for setting boundaries around her news consumption, but her bigger concern was how she would spend that hour or two each morning. What would she do instead? I could have recommended she buckle down and create some new healthy habits, like a meditation or journaling practice. But in the spirit of being gentle, I suggested she watch a fun movie or comedy show she enjoys (I would have gone with a Nancy Meyers movie, *The Holiday* or *It's Complicated*). She pushed back. Watch mindless TV during the day? How indulgent. That couldn't be right. I smiled.

Gentle suggestions are surprisingly hard to receive. We want to suffer. We *expect* to suffer. It's so hard to let go of our belief that you always get better results from hard work. I explained to Cally that at some point, she'd likely move on from watching her favorite movies or shows in the morning. Since she was already watching something (that made her feel like shit), the easiest shift would be to watch something else, preferably something that made her feel good. She didn't need an abundance of willpower to stop watching the news; she just needed to forget about it by watching something else. A few weeks later, she let me know she had been enjoying *Frasier* reruns. They made her laugh and they were only half an hour long. As a bonus, because she had already seen them before, they turned into background noise while she got ready for the day.

When we're changing a habit, or making a shift in our life, instead of getting ready to white-knuckle it (another tragic metaphor for suffering), we need to be asking questions like:

- What's the tiniest step I can take?
- Is there a gentler way?
- How can I make this easier?

Your brain will fight this line of questioning because somewhere in there you still believe that you need to get it done faster, that it should be uncomfortable, painful even, and, of course, that it should be really hard. And you'll have to remind yourself that if it's gentler, easier, or even better, if it feels good, it's more likely to last because it won't be something you think you have to do, it will be something you want to do.

During the early days of the pandemic, the news sucked me back in. At first it felt like survival but after weeks and months of hitting refresh several times a day to see what the number of daily COVID cases was, I knew my behavior was bordering on unhealthy. I created some rules and boundaries around my news consumption.

1. Only read the news (no videos).

    Watching the news impacts my nervous system differently than reading it. Videos, especially short, graphic clips on social media, plant themselves visually in my mind. When a trailer for a horror movie is on, I'm the lady who has to close her eyes, cover her ears, and murmur, "Nanananana." Otherwise, that trailer will reappear in my dreams. It's the same for news. When I read an article, it's easier to dissect what's important and leave the rest behind. You get to decide how you consume news. I choose what I let into my heart and soul and how I let it in.

2. No news notifications.

    Breaking-news notifications throughout the day are alarming and scary, and you don't need any part of it. If it's something you must know immediately, someone will tell you or you'll get a local news alert. CNN doesn't need to frighten you every hour.

3. Don't go looking for it.

    Instead of visiting news sites for my news, I subscribe to *The Skimm*. If I choose to open the daily email, I can see the headlines and a short summary, then decide if I want to know more. I usually do not.

4. Don't take the bait.

    When heated current events come up in conversation, don't take the bait. This might be the hardest one. There are some headlines that I don't want to discuss with some people or at certain times. I know it's not good for my mental health or relationships. Typically, I try to change the subject and divert the conversation, but this one is certainly a longer work in progress for me.

5. Take regular breaks from all news.

I really don't need to know about most of the news out there. Sometimes I need a full stop. No news, no social media, no outside opinions about the state of the world. I need a break. Whenever I share that I'm taking a break from the news, someone always tells me that it's important to stay informed, as if my news break is irresponsible. I agree that it's good to be informed. Kind of. It is important to stay informed but not on an hourly basis or even a daily basis. I also check in to see if being informed is helping me to take action (like calling my local representatives, signing a petition, or donating to a cause), if knowing certain things is moving me forward in some way, or if it is paralyzing me. If you are feeling overwhelmed, you can take a break from the news, social media, and the internet whenever you want. Being uninformed for a minute allows you to feel the way you want to feel, instead of living in a reactionary state 24/7.

WHY WE SHOULD BREAK UP
WITH BREAKING NEWS

- While it's breaking, news can be highly speculative and inaccurate. If you are looking to the news for reliable information, this isn't the time. Giving the news time to settle will help to avoid some unnecessary highs and lows.

- If you are minding their business, who's minding yours? Author and spiritual teacher Byron Katie says there are only three kinds of business in the universe: "mine, yours and God's."[2] When you are feeling lonely or hurt, you are likely in someone else's business. Katie says in a brief article on Awakin.org, "Much of our stress comes from mentally living out of our own business. When I think, 'You need to get a job, I want you to be happy, you should be on time, you need to take better care of yourself,' I am in your business. When I'm worried about earthquakes, floods, war, or when I will die, I am in God's business. If I am mentally in your business or in God's business, the effect is separation." In other words, if you are totally lost in the business of breaking news, who is taking care of what is meaningful and important to you? I know it's obvious, but the answer is: no one.

• Consuming breaking news is like getting on the scale. Unless you have a specific medical condition where your doctor recommends you weigh yourself, this practice is antiquated. How much you weigh or what news is breaking right now is unhelpful because it changes minute by minute. Yet it affects how we feel, usually in a negative way, which then affects how we move through our day and treat others. Breaking news equals stress. Stress can have a negative impact on mental and physical health and our relationships.

These days, it feels like all news is breaking news. There is such a fine line between being informed and becoming completely overwhelmed. If what we want (and need) in our lives is more peace and ease, we need to break up with breaking news.

The Tiny Steps

These tiny steps are here to help you break up with breaking news. If it feels hard, make it easier, smaller, and softer. You don't have to suffer through.

⁘ *Set clear boundaries.* Write down clear boundaries around news consumption for the next few days or weeks. If you want a daily news update, do it through email from your favorite source so you don't have to go to Google or a website full of more headlines that tempt you to click. Next, choose a time that works best for you. I recommend sometime between 10:00 a.m. and 2:00 p.m. because then you aren't beginning or ending your day with the news. If you can, include a full twenty-four to forty-eight hours a week with no news (or internet) at all. You'll be amazed by how much better you feel.

⁘ *Do for one person.* Podcast host and author Sharon McMahon says, "The antidote to despair is action. When you feel overwhelmed by bad news, instead of thinking about it nonstop like a hamster on a wheel or choosing to ignore it because you can't see a way to fix it and you're only one person, do something small and imperfect. Do for one person what you wish you could do for everyone...If we all do something small and imperfect, we will make far more change than waiting until the perfect plan appears."[3]

For example, we can:
- Deliver a meal to a neighbor.
- Hand out toiletries and sandwiches in our homeless communities.
- Contribute to a cause that matters to us.

⁘ *Notice catastrophizing.* I didn't even know this was a word until a few years ago, when a therapist called me out for doing it. Even when there is a catastrophe or hard things are going on, we can make it worse. We do this with our language, in the way we talk to our friends and family, and in how we allow our minds to carry us away with worst-case scenarios. We also catastrophize in the way we describe our own feelings. For example, instead of saying, "That was upsetting," we may say, "That destroyed me." Breaking news may encourage catastrophizing because, oftentimes, breaking news *is* catastrophizing. By not catastrophizing, you're not pretending hard things aren't happening. You're just recognizing that it's the wrong time to add fuel to the fire.

- ÷ *Donate.* When someone wants to debate a hot news topic to sway you or just to vent, change the subject and donate to the cause. For example, when *Roe v. Wade* was overturned and people wanted to debate, I donated to our local abortion fund. That made a bigger impact than arguing about something we weren't ever going to agree on.

- ÷ *Make a pact.* Ask friends and family for a news-free call. Agree to spend your next hang-out talking about something else if current events often come up. Another in-between option is to shift the conversation so that at least part of what you talk about focuses on something ordinary or sweet. Here are a few good questions to ask:
  - "What did you make for dinner?"
  - "Did anything happen recently that made you laugh?"
  - "What was something you enjoyed doing this week?"

During the pandemic, my friend Tammy and I would walk and talk. She lives in California and I live in Utah, so we'd arrange our calls when we could both be out for a walk. We'd compare notes on our local COVID situations and talk about different things going on in the news. Sometimes, we'd get a little carried away with the doom and gloom of COVID, wildfires, and politics, so we agreed to end our calls sharing a few things we were grateful for. That was our pact.

One Gentle Step

If you decided to skim through the tiny steps, try one gentle step. Change the channel. If you listen to news in your car, switch to music or silence. If Instagram is annoying you, log out. Make a gentle shift to something that soothes you.

Permission Slip:

I will not trade my peace for breaking news.

SEVEN

Go to Bed

Author and productivity expert Laura Vanderkam says that going to bed early is the way grown-ups sleep in. I could not agree more. And yet I often hear some version of the following from my clients: "I have too much to do. I stay up late getting things done." I know there are some very real problems around insomnia, but if you aren't getting enough sleep, one gentle first step you can take is to make sure you are putting yourself to bed at a similar time each night.

One of my clients, Alex, noticed that she was staying up later during the summer because the days were longer, and it got dark later. Once she decided to honor her usual bedtime of 9:00 p.m., she noticed that even though it was summer and still a little light outside, her dogs would always wind down easily. She decided to follow their lead and go to bed even though it wasn't dark yet. Once she was going to bed at almost the same time every night, she noticed that she was happier in the morning when she woke up. She said the sleep was helpful but having the routine and structure was also contributing to her mood boost. This said, many of us struggle with feeling like if we just get one more thing done we will rest easier.

THE MYTH OF DOING ONE MORE THING

If you struggle to sleep well, start with your bedtime. Are you going to bed at a reasonable hour, or are you staying up in the name of doing one more thing? It seems like there really is always one more thing to do, or at least that's what we tell ourselves. If you've ever hung around late at work or stayed up late at night to do one more thing so you wouldn't have to do it tomorrow, you understand the myth of doing one more thing. Each thing comes with the lie that it's the last thing of the day or the evening. Not only does one more thing lead to one more thing, but when you wake up the next day there is always one more thing. The interesting part is that we keep repeating this pattern, dismissing what we know because we are convinced that we'll get caught up if we just do ... one more thing.

Let's be honest: It's never only *one more thing* and it always takes longer than *just a sec*. How many times has someone interrupted you when you are doing a "quick" email check? You say, "Just a sec, I'm almost done"—and then twenty minutes later, you look up at them guiltily. Here's an idea: When you go to bed, leave the stress behind by creating a closing shift. My daughter introduced me to the idea of a closing shift. She started her closing shift because she discovered there was always more to do but she did not want to keep doing more—she wanted to go to bed! Most evenings when she's home, she wipes down her counters and brushes her teeth, and is then officially closed until the next day. This mini routine signals the end of her day. You can create your own closing shift to tell yourself it's the end of work or the end of your day. For instance, after work, make a list of three things to do in the morning, then set an autoresponder on your email. At home, wipe down all your counters and light a candle. Good job! Now you are closed. The doing part of the day is over. Sleep well.

Choose a reasonable bedtime for you. I like 9:00–9:30, but if you are used to staying up later, choose something before midnight, and something that will give you time to sleep for seven or eight hours. Once you commit to a bedtime, honor it. Even if you aren't falling asleep right away, create the gentle practice of putting yourself to bed at the time you choose. Read, or do something else that doesn't require a phone, TV, tablet, or computer. If you want to listen to a guided meditation or sleep sounds on your phone, that's OK—but no checking the weather (am I the only one who loves to check the weather?), social media, or anything else that may keep you over-stimulated and awake (*especially* not breaking news!). I know there may be some exceptions here, like if you work a night shift. But even then, you can do this routine when you get home. Leave the emails, extra house cleaning, and other tasks for another day.

At first, you may feel a little frustrated, especially if you struggle with something called Revenge Bedtime Procrastination. "We value productivity so much that we pack our days," says Lauren Whitehurst,[1] a cognitive neuroscientist and sleep researcher at the University of Kentucky. She says that revenge bedtime procrastination "is really a kind of commentary on [our lack of downtime.]" It's not about the *inability* to sleep; it's about delaying sleep in an effort to assert some kind of control over your time. It is possible that your restless nights start with your refusal to go to bed in the first place. There could be a connection, and there is only one way to find out. Go to bed.

Remember little Courtney from earlier? She didn't want to nap. She didn't want to go to bed early, either. She thought that after she fell asleep, everyone would be having fun without her. Now, she does not care. As an adult, I find myself looking forward to all the things my younger self thought were a punishment. While I hated it when I was five, ten, and even twenty, I now love napping, going home early, and putting myself to bed on time. Those are all little gifts I give myself.

The Tiny Steps

These tiny steps will help you honor your bedtime and start to get the sleep and deeper rest you need.

- ⁕ *Set an alarm.* Don't count on remembering your bedtime every night, especially when you are getting started. Set an alarm on your phone thirty minutes before you want to go to bed. Then set another for five minutes before. Make this process annoying enough that you have to respond by going to bed.

- ⁕ *Notice if putting yourself to bed on time makes a difference.* Each morning, jot down a couple of words about what it felt like to go to bed on time and how you slept. Do this for a few weeks so you can see the pattern instead of trying to remember how you felt each day during this shift. If writing every morning feels like too much, rate your sleep 1–5 (1 = waking up after a spotty night of sleep, and 5 = waking up feeling refreshed and rested). See if your numbers increase with some practice. Don't give up after a few days; this takes time.

- ⁕ *Identify what disrupts your sleep.* Aside from doing more things, what else gets between you and a good night's sleep? Some of the usual suspects include caffeine, alcohol, screens, and worrying. Some of these are easier to remove than others. But where you can, try limiting your access to these things a few hours before you go to bed. When you remove some of the mystery of why you can't sleep, it may be easier to sleep.

- ❖ *Promise to do it tomorrow.* Right before we fall asleep, we love to review everything we didn't get done or worry about problems we can't fix in that moment. If these things pop up and you are mentally writing a list on your ceiling, put it on paper instead. If that's too hard, record an audio note. If you don't know what to say, try a version of this: "I can't fall asleep because the following things are on my mind. Here's a quick list. If I wake up still worried, I'll listen to this and see if anything still needs my attention." Promise to do the thing, worry about it, or think about how to fix it tomorrow. Write it down, fold up the paper, and then, if you aren't bothered in the morning by any of the things that seemed so pressing right before bed, throw the paper out.
- ❖ *Tear your to-do list in half.* If you tend to go overboard with your daily list of to-dos, this tiny step is a great way to get it all done. Make your to-do list in order of priority and do what you can comfortably do within waking hours. Next, rip the list in half and keep the items you didn't get to for the next day—or ask yourself: Can you just throw out the bottom part of the list because those things weren't really that important after all?

One Gentle Step

If you are too tired from not sleeping to do the tiny steps, here is one gentle step. Go to bed on time just for tonight. One night, one time.

Permission Slip:

Going to bed is more important than doing one more thing.

EIGHT

Find Connection

Even though the stereotypical way to rest looks like someone lying down in bed, there are many ways to rest. One Monday afternoon, my friend and corporate storytelling coach Marsha Shandur was shaken up, trying to process a horrific world event that was happening. She wanted to stay informed and felt like she couldn't look away. But being unable to tear herself away from social media and breaking news wasn't helping her take effective action. On the contrary, she became overwhelmed, incapable of anything but scrolling. She messaged me, "The news is taking me down right now," and we brainstormed some ideas to help her feel better. The very next day she told me, "After we spoke, it was obvious I needed to feel my feelings, so I had a big sobbing cry on my bed. Then I realized I had to get out of that hole before I could do anything."

That evening she was hosting her live storytelling show in Toronto, which required her to connect with a bunch of storytellers and hundreds of audience members. As an extrovert, this not only provided her with connection, it was also fun for her. Dr. Stuart Brown, the founder of the National Institute of Play, says that "the opposite of fun isn't work, it's depression." Later, Marsha told me that for her, connection + play = rest because it replenishes her. When she falls down an emotional hole like that, connection and play bring her back. That's how she rests. She felt much better and, because of that, was able to take action in a meaningful way about the situation, something she hadn't been capable of the day before. She filled her cup and had something to give back. Even though nothing around her had changed, something within her changed.

Just like there is more than one way to rest, there is more than one way to connect, too. Connecting with others may fill your cup. There are also ways you can connect to your own body to shift the way you feel. I've learned so much over the years from my friend, therapist Rachel Shanken.[1] She practices talk therapy and somatic therapy at her New York City practice, called MindBodyWise. She shared with me some easy body movements to help shift your mood. Things like standing taller, loosening your jaw, dropping your shoulders, or opening your arms. It sounds so simple and it works. Not only can these movements shift your mood but somatic therapy can be especially effective in treating trauma, PTSD, anxiety, and depression. Here's how *Psychology Today* defines somatic therapy: "Somatic therapy is a form of body-centered therapy that looks at the connection of mind and body and uses both psychotherapy and physical therapies for holistic healing. In addition to talk therapy, somatic therapy practitioners use mind-body exercises and other physical techniques to help release the pent-up tension that negatively affects a patient's physical and emotional wellbeing."[2]

Some examples of somatic therapy include breathing exercises, mindfulness practices, and dance. Calandra Balfour, a UK-based trauma-informed practitioner, explains, "The goal of somatic therapy is to help individuals release emotional and physical trauma that is stored in the body."[3] My friend Rachel has often said, "Our issues are in our tissues." While healing from trauma is a worth-while journey and can dramatically affect your overall wellness, in this chapter we are just going to focus on simple ways to connect your body with your mind. We see examples of how they are con-nected all the time, like when you catch a cold after a busy week or stressful time, or how your back or neck can sometimes hurt after a challenging conversation. While this mind-body connec-tion is available to us, most of us have experienced a disconnect between the two, which could have been caused by anything from a trauma to taking care of everyone but ourselves. Sometimes it's hard to identify exactly where the disconnect comes from because we don't store that memory in our working minds. Instead, it lives in our bodies.

MIND-BODY PRACTICES

Do a body scan. Rachel suggests a mind-body scan. She says, "Pause to notice what you're feeling in your body. I like to scan starting with my toes and moving all the way up, part by part, and tuning in. No need to judge what you notice. No need to change anything. Just noticing is hugely calming for your whole system." Make this a simple ritual by setting a two- to five-minute timer for the whole scan. To go further with your mind-body connection, you can find out more about Rachel's work at mindbodywise.com.

Put your hands on your heart before you put them on your phone. Earlier I mentioned a heart practice, which you can incorporate here. More important, though, is the timing or sequence. Heart before phone. Before you touch your phone, anytime, place your hands on your heart, or one hand on your heart and one hand on your belly. By making a mind-body connection first, you are checking in with yourself before you check out into whatever dopamine hits await on your phone. You are sending a signal that you come first, that you are more important to you than anything you'll find in your feed. When you want real connection and honest answers, check your heart more than you check your phone.

Activate your senses. See how your mind and body interact when you smell something. According to some studies,[4] the scent of citrus can help the body produce the happy hormone serotonin. My friend Tessa would disagree—she doesn't like the smell of oranges at all. Like all of these gentle practices and tiny steps, don't forget to do what works best for you. I know the smell of coffee in the morning makes me feel more awake. Try noticing what's going on with your other senses, too. When you see something lovely, how do your mind and body react? What about when you taste something salty? Have you ever been surprised by a loud noise and actually felt it in your body, as if your heart fell into your belly? Starting to be aware of those moments will give you a chance to notice how intertwined your body and mind really are.

Follow your breath. Take a deep breath and follow it with your mind. Where does it go? Can you feel your rib cage, or your belly, expand? If you can, try to direct your breath into another part of your body. I remember yoga teachers telling me to breathe into my toes or hands, and at first, I didn't understand so I practiced. I took a breath and imagined it coming in and then spreading throughout my body. Whether that was happening physiologically or not wasn't important. The magic that was happening was me feeling my own mind-body connection. I learned how to use something like breathing (which we often take for granted) to calm me down or bring me back to the present instead of getting taken down when something challenging happens.

Knowing that we can rest in other ways allows us to come back to ourselves in most situations instead of having to wait until we climb in bed at the end of the day. We are so powerful in our ability to rescue ourselves from overwhelm, fear, and uncertainty. It doesn't mean we ignore these feelings or that they aren't happening for legitimate reasons. Instead, it means that we can better address them. Rest—whatever that looks like for us—is almost always available to us.

The Tiny Steps

These tiny steps will help you recognize and strengthen your mind-body connection so you can experience the benefits of this harmonious relationship more often. For deeper work, consider working with a therapist or somatic therapy practitioner.

- *Identify your power.* Notice a recent mind-body connection. Think back over the last few days. Remember how you felt after smelling coffee brewing, or when someone surprised you with a knock at the door. Where did you feel it in your body? Or, when you got a little too cold or too hot, how did that affect your thoughts?
- *Make a list of what feels restful to you.* Now that you know rest comes in many forms, what feels restful to you? Reading a book may feel restful, or connecting with friends. Sometimes it's *how* we do something that feels restful. For instance, when I'm cooking dinner on a Wednesday, it's not restful. But if I'm making soup on a Saturday afternoon with my favorite music playing, that relaxes me and feels like a gentle rest. Start to experiment with the things on your list so you can employ these activities when you need them most.

⚡ *Rest in the moment.* We are so used to pushing through difficult situations that sometimes it's days or weeks before we
actually come down to earth and rest. The next time you
are about to push through, ask yourself, "Is there something I can do to rest through?" You can consult your list,
or simply take a few deep breaths.

One Gentle Step

If you are feeling especially disconnected from your body,
these tiny steps may not be tiny enough. Instead, try the
gentle step. Take one of Rachel's suggestions and simply
drop your shoulders or loosen your jaw.

Permission Slip:

I can rest the way I want to rest.

NINE

Redefine Your Guilt

It was a Monday morning, and I was feeling really guilty. In an attempt to shift that, I decided to go for a walk around the lake near my house, but it didn't work. I had just quit my job and started my own business, and this was the first Monday morning that I didn't have to go into the office for another torturous sales meeting. As I walked along the pebble-covered path, my thoughts were running wild. *Why aren't I feeling my usual Monday morning angst? Shouldn't I be working hard and dreading the rest of the week? It's Monday morning...isn't this GO GO GO time?! Shouldn't this be harder? Shouldn't I be at my desk instead of out for a walk?* After several days of going for a morning walk and thinking thoughts like this, I finally realized something: I wasn't feeling guilt, I was feeling uncomfortable. I was taking really good care of myself and I wasn't used to doing that, so I was experiencing some discomfort. It took some time, but I did stop feeling bad on those walks. Instead, I started feeling healthy, rested, and free.

If you feel guilty for working less, slowing down, and considering something new for yourself, consider that it might not be justified guilt. You might just feel uncomfortable getting what it is you know you need to thrive in your life. Here is a list of some of the things you will likely lose out on if you don't redefine your guilt:

- **Time.** When you commit to something just because you feel guilty, you're stealing time from your favorite people and projects.
- **Energy.** If you are low on energy and say yes to a new project out of guilt, consider the fact that what you are doing is not feeding your heart and soul. If you are working on something that you feel excited about, you will feel excitement. If you are working on something that you feel miserable about, you will feel miserable and it will drain your energy even further.
- **Money.** Have you ever made a purchase because you felt you should? *She bought me that, so I should buy her this. We are going there for a party, so we should buy them that. I treated him poorly so I should buy him one of those. They might not know how much we love them, so let's get them this.* Stop it. Your presents don't equal love. Your presence does.
- **Real joy.** If you are spending your time, energy, or money doing something out of guilt, you'll miss an opportunity to do something you actually love, something that makes your heart swell, something that will bring you and the world real joy. Do not miss out on real joy. It's amazing.

We let guilt prevent us from resting, loving, and living the way we want to live. How many times have you gone to work when you were sick because you felt too guilty to take care of yourself? Or, have you ever beaten yourself up because you felt guilty for not doing enough, or for doing nothing? We'll talk more about this in part 2, "Less," but if you spend time doing nothing and feeling guilty the whole time, what was the point? Usually, the problem is not feeling a bit of guilt. The problem is when you let your feeling of guilt guide you. For instance, say you have an hour in the middle of the day, and you decide to go for a walk and listen to your favorite podcast. But if your guilt is so distracting that you can't pay attention to the walk or the podcast, then you'll come back from the walk feeling not only guilty but frustrated and anxious, too.

We have to stop with the guilt. Giving it so much attention is only reinforcing the idea that we aren't worthy of feeling the way we want to feel. It's suggesting that being in our lives the way we are isn't good enough. That guilt is all rooted in our patriarchal capitalist upbringing, which insists we prove our worth by constantly doing more, producing more, going harder, and never stopping. Until we do stop, we won't have the room to rest or fully enjoy our lives. You can stop now. It's OK.

The Tiny Steps

These tiny steps will help you identify what you are really feeling. Just because you've always held on to guilt doesn't mean you have to keep holding on to guilt. It's worth considering that you've suffered enough.

- *Ask yourself about your guilt.* Before assuming you feel guilty, ask, "Is this guilt or is this discomfort?" Inherent to the idea of guilt is that you've done something wrong. Usually you haven't done anything wrong. Instead, you feel guilty when you don't think you got *enough* done, or when you have to say no or set a boundary with someone you love. You may even feel guilty when you get sick and have to take time off or rest. People tell me they feel guilty for relaxing and doing nothing, or not attending an event they don't want to attend. If you can relate and have felt guilty for these things, perhaps it's not guilt. Instead, you are feeling discomfort for taking care of yourself.

✢ *Notice where it shows up.* When your guilty feeling shows up, how does it show up? Where is it in your body? For instance, when you can't release the pressure to do more or push through, notice the actual tension. Where is it? Can you feel it in your body? Is it in your jaw, neck, or hands, or somewhere else? Identify the physical manifestation and then soften it, relax it, keep releasing it.

✢ *Apologize.* Maybe your guilt is justifiable guilt for doing something you wish you hadn't. It may be time to apologize to someone, then forgive yourself for being human. Even if you think you waited too long, put it out there. It's never too late to do better and be kinder. (Note: Even if your apology isn't accepted or doesn't fix a problem, it still has value. This isn't about controlling someone else's behavior or responses—you can't do that. This is about setting things right with *yourself.*)

✢ *Remember: Feeling guilty for taking care of yourself is not taking care of yourself.* Give yourself a guilt-free pass to go to bed early, say no to an invitation, or take care in the way you need to take care.

One Gentle Step

If you've been carrying guilt for a while, you may not feel like doing any of the tiny steps. Instead release the hold guilt has on you for a moment by engaging in something that makes you laugh. Watch a funny movie, call a friend who always makes you smile, or pull up in your mind a memory of something funny that happened to you.

Replace your guilt with some lighthearted laughter, even just for a moment.

Permission Slip:

It's OK to say goodbye to guilt when it's not serving me.

TEN

The New Rules
for Rest

The old rules tell us we have to earn our rest. They say we must demonstrate and prove our need to rest and relax, either because we've worked hard or because our health is failing. If you've done it all, or you can't do anything...*then* you can rest. Oh, and you are allowed to relax on vacation for two weeks a year, if you are privileged and lucky (and are willing to check your email thirty times a day). I've had people tell me they prefer to work through their vacations so that when they get home, they don't have to come back to extra work to catch up on. Come to think of it, I even "check in" during time off. There was one time, though, when I went to my favorite little beach town in California, when I promised myself I'd stay completely off the internet for eight long days. I say "long" because, without the constant inflow of information, the days were longer, my mind was clearer, my surroundings were brighter, and it made me want even more time off.

We deserve to enjoy guilt-free rest, at any time of the year. It's time to reject the unspoken, old rules...so I made us new ones.

The new rules of rest

1. Thou shalt read at least a few pages of a good book or listen to relaxing music and enjoy a cup of tea before checking email or social media in the morning.
2. Thou shalt take a nap or a bath long before there is a check mark next to every single thing on thine to-do list.
3. Thou shalt not wait for the weekend to rest or for a vacation to relax.
4. Thou shalt not apologize for resting and relaxing.
5. Before finishing the dishes or cleaning up the house, thou shalt watch an episode of *Gilmore Girls* or go for a walk.
6. Thou shalt ease through hard days instead of pushing through them.
7. When people tell thee, "No pain, no gain" or "I'm so busy" or "I can sleep when I'm dead," thou shalt gently tell people to eff off or simply smile and share this book with them.
8. Thou shalt use free time to be free, not to catch up (and there shalt be no worrying about catching up after rest and relaxation).
9. Thou shalt not compare thine productivity or busyness to the productivity or busyness of others, understanding that it only glorifies the thing that is tearing us down and wearing us out.
10. Thou shalt relax and claim thine rest as a right not a reward.

These new rules are here to help you see rest differently. It's not a treat or a reward. It's literally necessary for your physical and mental health and will do wonders for your relationships and creativity, too.

Let's dig a little deeper and unpack these rules.

1. **Thou shalt read at least a few pages of a good book or listen to relaxing music and enjoy a cup of tea before checking email or social media in the morning.** Email, social media, the weather app, and other things you might check are a quick escape and bit of numbing. When you don't know what to do, you might mindlessly go to them. Instead, put a sticky note on your phone with this first commandment.
2. **Thou shalt take a nap or a bath long before there is a check mark next to every single thing on thine to-do list.** Rest and relaxation are just as important as the other things on your to-do list (if not more). You don't have to get everything else done first, mostly because everything else will never be done. Stop saving rest until later—put it at the top of your to-do list!
3. **Thou shalt not wait for the weekend to rest or for a vacation to relax.** Just like it's hard to make up for lost sleep, you can't get all the benefits of regular rest and relaxation with a quick hit on Saturday morning or even by taking a full week or two off. Rest must be a regular practice. If it's not, you'll spend most of your vacation trying to figure out how not to be so stressed out. By the time you take your first relaxing breath, you'll be packing up to go home.
4. **Thou shalt not apologize for resting and relaxing.** Also, no prioritizing other people's expectations of your schedule and productivity. They don't get a vote. The only voice or vote that matters here is yours. If your voice says rest, trust it. No apology required.
5. **Before finishing the dishes or cleaning up the house, thou shalt watch an episode of *Gilmore Girls* or go for a walk.** Here we go again with that feeling of needing to get

everything done before you can relax. If you won't rest until everything is picture perfect, only to discover that by the time you have everything done you've run out of time to relax, please see what the problem is here. You are allowed to enjoy yourself even when there are dinner dishes still in the sink. If you absolutely can't do this, try paper plates for a while.

6. **Thou shalt ease through hard days instead of pushing through them.** Just because you *can* push through doesn't mean it's the best choice. It's usually the worst choice. For instance, going to work sick keeps you sick longer, makes your work harder, and gets everyone around you sick. I used to think that I was strong for pushing through. I thought I was good at it and that by doing it constantly I was getting stronger. In reality, the opposite was happening. I was wearing myself down, exhausting my body and my mind. Finally, I couldn't push through anymore. When I started resting through instead, I realized I'd had it all wrong. I didn't have to rush my healing, hide my pain, or find an immediate solution. Choose to ease through. You are allowed.

7. **When people tell thee, "No pain, no gain" or "I'm so busy" or "I can sleep when I'm dead," thou shalt gently tell people to eff off or simply smile and share this book with them.** No wonder we always feel pressure to do more. Everyone is always talking about their toxic productivity. Tell them, "No thank you." We don't become happier, more fulfilled, and connected by working hard, playing hard, going above and beyond, and pushing through. Instead, we end up depleted, uninspired, sick, tired, and overwhelmed. It's time for a new path forward.

8. **Thou shalt use free time to be free, not to catch up (and there shalt be no worrying about catching up after rest and relaxation).** If catching up worked, you'd be caught up by now. Stop giving up your free time to the myth of "catching up."

9. **Thou shalt not compare thine productivity or busyness to the productivity or busyness of others, understanding that it only glorifies the thing that is tearing us down and wearing us out.** Let's stop telling each other how busy we are. It's not helping. It makes us feel like we have to keep doing more to measure up.

10. **Thou shalt relax and claim thine rest as a right not a reward.** This one needs no elaboration. Like Karlee Flores said about one of the days in her Gentle January, "I didn't need to deserve today. I took it for myself. And it felt great."

The old rules are outdated and over. It's time for us to rest and relax in the ways that we want and need to rest and relax. By doing that, we'll encourage each other to rest, to go to bed on time, and to do that "one more thing" another time. Use these rules or write your own to remind yourself how important it is to prioritize rest in your life.

The Tiny Steps

These tiny steps will encourage you to embrace a few of these new rules or to make your own.

❖ *Catch yourself catching up.* When you notice that you are trying to catch up, remind yourself that this is just another time myth, like falling behind and getting ahead. It's a myth or a game that keeps you running in circles.

- *Create your own rules.* Adjust these rules to fit your own seasons and lifestyle. Make them work for you, starting right now. This is another great way to practice trusting yourself.
- *Ask questions.* If you are trying to figure out how to carry your new rules into your day-to-day life, answer the following questions:
  - What is the gentlest thing I can do for myself in this moment? Like, right now?
  - How can I feel love and gratitude for the exact next thing I have to do without worrying about all of the other steps that follow?
  - What would help me relax into where I am right now?
  - Can I stop trying to figure everything out and just sit still for a bit?

One Gentle Step

Choose one restful activity. Have something top of mind to do instead of pushing through. Maybe it's a book, a TV show, a walk, or a favorite snack. Make a note somewhere of what the restful thing is so you don't have to figure it out when you are exhausted.

Permission Slip:

I reject the old rules of rest and will embrace my own rules.

A LITTLE MORE ON REST

You may notice that not every gentle practice resonates with you or interests you at all. The goal when navigating these sections is to consider the recommendations and do what works best for you. If you can reach a thoughtful state of rest only by trying one idea out of ten, that's great. Within this gentle work you will likely benefit from doing less instead of more.

Even though this section on rest is coming to an end, you can be in a season of rest anytime. It may take months of dedicating time to or prioritizing rest; in many cases, it's shorter than that. Between work, family, and other parts of life, your rest may come in smaller doses. It may feel challenging to make room for rest. Remember when I said we'd talk about what to do when things aren't easy? Being gentle, doing the tiny steps or even the gentle step, isn't always going to be easy, but you can always choose to make it easier. If making a change feels hard, make it softer. When you read a suggestion and immediately think, *Huh, easier said than done*, it's easy to dismiss the idea altogether. Instead, find a milder way, an easier path, or a gentler step. Keep coming back to the idea that you don't have to push through. Perhaps you can ease through instead.

Here's an example: You want to declutter your closet, but it feels impossible given your current situation (maybe your closet is a mess, or you don't have the time and energy needed for a complete overhaul). You could say, "Easier said than done," and give up before you even start. *Or* you could make the change feel softer and easier. Instead, you could commit to five minutes a day of removing things you never wear.

You may resist rest when you need it the most. If your tendency is to try to escape discomfort and rush into a solution, rest may not be part of your natural equation. Before trying to fix things or figure out next steps, before taking on something new or throwing yourself into a new self-help strategy, how about just resting? Give yourself space to be slow and soft and to come back to you. From there, you can take more effective action.

Before you move into part 2, "Less," consider taking time to rest. This is the third time I've gently invited you to put this book down and rest. It may help to remember how rest encourages the Gentle You. Remember that rest contributes to your health, ability to focus, and creative flow. Although you now have a clear understanding of why rest is important as well as some practical strategies to help you rest, we still have to cheer each other on and gently remind each other that now is a great time to rest. In fact, waiting for a better time might be a mistake. Even if it feels restful and relaxing to read (I know it usually does for me), stop the input of new information, and give your brain and body a little time to renew and reset. It might be ten minutes, like we talked about in chapter 1. Maybe you are ready to rest longer than that and let yourself doze off. Wherever you are right now, take some amount of rest for yourself.

If you don't feel ready to move on to the next section, ask yourself what one gentle step might be. Is it time to reread this section and stay in the season of rest? Or time to initiate some conversations with family members about some of the things you've learned and want to practice? Maybe the next gentle step is to reach out to me with any questions (support@bemorewithless.com). Continue to take tiny steps that bring you closer and closer to the Gentle You.

PART II

LESS

I used to fill my life with more when I felt stressed out and over-whelmed. I really believed that more was the solution. When money was a problem, I tried to find more, make more, and spend more. When relationships were a problem, I had to give more, do better, and work harder to prove my love. When pain was a prob-lem, I needed more pain relief in the form of shopping or Chardon-nay. When I say pain, I mean the pain of boredom or frustration, the pain of doing work I didn't enjoy or spending time with people I didn't really want to spend time with. I kept trying to fix my pain with more, never thinking that more was contributing to the pain. The idea of sitting with my feelings didn't occur to me. But more never solved my problems; it only led to more problems. When I started to experiment with less, I realized that *this* was what my heart had been craving. Less stuff, less debt, less chaos, less distrac-tion, and fewer decisions. When you are stressed, overwhelmed, and exhausted, the answer is usually less. Get rid of something, or lots of somethings. Now, when I'm feeling stressed out or anxious,

I look around. I notice the space in my home, on my to-do list and planner, and in my inboxes. When things are a little too full around me, they get a little too full within me. I know it's time to let go. Something has to give, or lots of somethings. More may equal more, but less equals more, too. Less stuff equals more space. Less busyness equals more time. Less chaos equals more calm. Less stress equals more ease. The Gentle You doesn't want more for the sake of more; she wants more of the good stuff. This is how we take care.

"Rest" is the first section of this book, but in my life the first step toward the Gentle Me was "Less." Making space and time for what mattered to me was the beginning of my healing journey. Prioritizing less over more was how I began to question everything I thought and how I learned how to take care of myself. At first it was about clearing stress so I could live well with MS. Then less became even more. I moved from decluttering and paying off debt to looking at how I moved through the world and through my life. I saw how disconnected I was. I saw how rushing through the day, pinging from thing to thing, made it impossible to really be *in* my life. With so much going on, the name of the game had become "getting as much done as possible." I discovered that I was doing this at the cost of noticing how I felt in my life. I was accumulating experiences without actually experiencing them.

When I prioritized the idea of noticing what was going on in my life and showing up for it, I began to differentiate between things that mattered to me and things that did not. On the days I was too busy to notice or show up, I knew something was up. Why was I removed from myself? What had taken me from feeling like I was navigating life and made me feel more like life was navigating me? Sometimes, it was something outside of my control, like an unexpected meeting, getting sick, a fire to put out at work, or a global pandemic. Most of the time, it was me. It was me saying yes to one more thing, me overreacting, or me forgetting to prioritize *me*. This was usually a case of tasks or actions I'd agreed to slowly and quietly building up.

At first, I didn't have the clarity to see that I was overwhelmed until after it had already happened. Now, with lots of practice and curiosity, I can usually see overwhelm coming. When I begin to sense that feeling creeping around, I look at what in my life (or my head) is building up and is about to become too much. Then I know that the answer is not more, it's less. I'll share some examples in the gentle practices in this section, so you can assess whether something you decide to do is standing in the way of or adding value to your life, helping you in some way. If it's the latter, great; if it's the former, it's time to focus on less.

I'm interested in less overall. But more important to me is that we focus on adding more space and time for things in our lives that add value. The only way is to create room to pay attention. Otherwise, it's too noisy to know what is helping and what isn't.

Sometimes we think of "less" as a sacrifice. I've found it to be a great privilege. Not only that, but I am privileged to choose what I own, what I give my attention to, how I spend my time, what I let in my life, and who gets my energy. I do not take any of that for granted because I know that there are people without that option. That same privilege applies to my ability to choose what I release from my life, from clutter and debt to thoughts and opinions that don't serve me (especially my own). This gift has always been available to me, even when I was scrambling to make ends meet and raising my daughter as a single mom, but I'm not exaggerating when I tell you that I had literally no idea about simplicity, minimalism, privilege, or how to change my life. Back then, my definition of success was having a life that was bigger and better than the one I had, and my definition of "bigger and better" was almost entirely about the things I owned and the things I wanted.

Fast-forward to a new marriage and a chance to start again, and I still held the bigger, better, more vision. Enter lifestyle creep. I was earning more but spending more, still in just as much debt, craving a bigger closet and nicer furniture. So of course, I bought a big house with a mortgage that had obscene terms. If you don't think our systems hold us back, try getting a mortgage when your credit score is in the trash. Not even a year later, soon after my diagnosis, I began to heal. I began to learn and understand that I didn't need more stuff, more closet space, or more shoes. I didn't want a bigger life full of things I didn't have the time or energy to enjoy. What I needed, what I wanted, what I truly craved was less.

Each of the gentle practices in the "Less" section will give you an opportunity to explore what "enough" means to you. It's natural to try and define and measure "enough" from a place of lack. I used to worry about having enough money to pay the bills, enough time to spend with my daughter, enough calm to sleep through the night, and enough strength to acquire all that more I was looking for. I think that was probably why I always thought I needed more. I feel like this is a common story: People who have struggled with believing they have enough (or are enough) think that having more will soothe that pain. Of course, it doesn't and so then you've created a home or a career or a life that you never really wanted in the first place.

Back in the "more" days, as I was making decisions for my life, I didn't have these realizations. Most of us don't. We're too busy looking forward, wondering what's next or looking back, wondering what we could have done differently. We're too busy being busy to actually be present. Add to that the constant pressure of being a human and it's no wonder we get confused, lost, and convinced that we need something more to feel better. Oh yeah, and then no one talks openly about these feelings, so instead we all think we're falling behind, failing at doing the life thing right.

Making the "enough" decision is an ongoing conversation. It changes as your life changes. It changes as *you* change. There isn't one right answer for everyone. There isn't even one right answer for today you or the five-years-ago you or the five-years-from-now you. The best way to begin the conversation with yourself is to notice when you feel like you need more. For instance, when you have a really crappy day at work and you want something (more) to lift you up. What do you pick up to numb that crap day? A new pair of shoes, a cocktail, some takeout? Maybe busyness is your drug of choice, so you fill your weekend with too much work or too many errands or events. Are any of those things terrible on their own? No! I just ordered takeout last night. What makes them a problem is when they are a reaction instead of an intentional decision. Once you begin to engage in considering what you really want and really need, and where that falls on the more/less/enough scale, you'll be living a more intentional life.

Speaking of making decisions, living a life with fewer things means fewer decisions. This means less decision fatigue. Because of some general rules I've created for myself around the same decisions that I have to make every day, I don't have to constantly rethink what I want to do. This is a successful practice most of the time. I do like to break the rules sometimes. Occasionally I'll break a rule on a whim but usually it's because a rule isn't working anymore. I won't hold on to a rule or an idea just because I used to think it was a good idea. Creating some rules might help you, too. For example, when my husband and I were decluttering, instead of getting weighed down by the decisions we'd have to make, like what to sell and what to donate, we decided on this rule: Anything that would be worth $50 or more gets sold, and everything else we donate. With that one rule, we eliminated hundreds of decisions. My rules are subject to change (autonomy and all that) but here they are.

1. Get up and go to bed about the same time every day. If I know that I'll be waking up at 6:00 a.m. and getting in bed at 9:00 p.m. every day, I don't have to argue with myself about it and bargain with my snooze button or that one more thing that is begging to get done before I go to bed. Instead of focusing on how much sleep I get, I know that a regular sleep schedule will ensure that I have enough time to sleep well.

2. Start the day with meditation. While I do have a morning routine with other practices, the only nonnegotiable is that I start the day with meditation. Yep, even before coffee. I usually do it twice a day for twenty minutes, but my rule is to meditate at least once a day, first thing.

3. Remove myself from conversations when I'm being mistreated. My teenage angst is long gone, so I won't subject myself to drama or any kind of abusive behavior. I don't need to fight back, prove that I'm right, or change anyone else. I only need to decide how I behave and what I am willing to tolerate.

4. Rest when I'm tired. You may have seen this one coming after reading the first section. I do not push through anymore. Sometimes I catch myself mid-push-through. This rule reminds me that even though I'm human and forget what works best for me, I can change my mind and course of action anytime.

5. I don't give up on myself. I may give up on a moment by resting when I'm tired or let go of something that isn't working for me, but I don't give up on myself. This means I keep coming back to the habits that are important to me, I keep opening to the Gentle Me, and I continue to change the way I change.

These rules aren't meant to boss me around or turn me into a robot. Quite the opposite. They reward me by removing decisions, so I have more mental clarity for my day and the other forty-two thousand decisions that await me. Some people go further or get more specific. Neuroscientist Moran Cerf always chooses the second item on the specials menu, no matter the dish. He told *Business Insider*, "Sometimes it's a big failure, but sometimes it's also a big failure when I choose myself."[1] He sees that both ways of choosing a menu item come with the same risk, so why not minimize the decision-making involved? He chooses from the specials menu because it's shorter than the full menu. Because of his specialty in researching brain functions around decisions, he likes to reserve more brainpower for bigger decisions. This works for him but not for everyone. I will repeat outfits, but I won't leave my lunch up to chance. As always, the trick is to find what works for *you*.

At the end of each year, I reflect on what I want to hold on to and what I want to let go of. That intentional reflection allows me to consider which of the new things I've picked up seem like a good addition and which feel like dead weight. From stuff, ideas, and projects to commitments, expectations, and goals, I remind myself that I won't hold on to something just because I used to think it was a good idea. Letting go of things is a process, of course. We've carried some of those things for so long that we forget how glorious the lightness is when we carry less. As I release things, I sleep better, laugh more often, and open my heart back up for more of what's waiting for me in the world. It's a relief to release the things I've been dragging along. Maybe they were dragging me.

As you consider the following gentle practices, remember the Gentle Way. Get clear about why you want to make a change, break it into tiny steps, and create a support system to encourage your progress. Keep coming back to the basics and leading with the Gentle You. Not every recommendation will resonate with you. Some will challenge you. Some may require some modification to make it work better for you. Others will be an easy yes, as is. Keep checking in with what works for you.

ONE

Home Release

To be clear, home release does not mean that you have to release your whole home (unless you want to), just most of the stuff inside of it. Even though we've established that less is about so much more than your stuff, starting with the tangible things will help you begin to enjoy the benefits of less. This can then help you be more open to other ways that living with less can be beneficial. If at any time the home release or other practices become overwhelming or you run out of time or energy, revisit the "Rest" section. As you continue to cultivate and connect with the Gentle You, it's very likely you will shift back and forth between "Rest" and "Less"—do what feels right for you.

While I usually recommend a slow and steady approach to decluttering (especially if you are decluttering for good, instead of the usual spring clean to make room for more stuff from Target), we are going to move more quickly this time. The benefit of slow and steady is that you remove any deadline pressures and have plenty of time to learn why you have so much stuff in the first place. The downside is that you also have plenty of time to overthink everything. That means time to question if you might need that thing "just in case," and time to procrastinate. In other words, time to talk yourself out of letting go.

One more note on why this quick home release is so important: My guess is you aren't reading this book to learn how to declutter. I didn't write it to teach you how to declutter. The focus is learning how to be gentle with yourself, and you need room for that. Creating space is essential for prioritizing the changes you want to make. This focus on being gentle is something new that will take time, energy, and attention. You can't just pile it on to everything else you have going on. First you have to remove some of the other stuff. Think about this anytime you feel moved to add something, especially if you are in a place where your things feel like enough or too much. Adding without subtracting is just bad life math. Too much + more stuff = overwhelm. Even good things are more things, and they require more space.

So let's get started on this quick and decisive room-by-room home release. If you don't have some of these rooms (or you have more rooms than these), adjust this list as necessary.

HOME RELEASE ROAD MAP

Prep: Gather bags and boxes. Fill up a water bottle (the one you want to hold on to). Make a playlist or get one from the Gentle Resources page on my website. Decide how long your first session is going to be. I recommend keeping your first session short, probably half the time you think you want to spend. Set a timer for your first break. Celebrate your decision to give the home release a go. You don't have to wait until you are finished to celebrate. Getting started is something to celebrate. Choose a celebration that allows you to acknowledge your progress. It might be baking cupcakes, watching your favorite show, or calling someone you love to say,

"Yay, guess what I did?!" Set the tone and get yourself ready to go with a little celebration.

Connect with your team: If you have help from friends or family, get together and spend fifteen minutes or so answering the following questions. If you don't have a team, answer them yourself. Why are we getting rid of as much stuff as possible today? Where do we put things we aren't sure about? What do we do if we feel frustrated, stressed, or stuck? Is there anything we can do to make this more fun? For instance, if we collectively release a hundred items, can we watch our favorite movie and eat pizza on the floor tonight? Assign a space where the outgoing stuff is going to live until you move it out of your home. Keep this area as contained as possible so you can begin to enjoy the space you are creating immediately—like maybe inside a closet, or even inside a box. Remind each other or yourself that this is not time to organize or reminisce. This is time to release as much stuff as possible to make room for . . . well, for anything you want.

Kitchen: This is the room that is notorious for duplicates and multiples. Seriously, how many coffee cups, water bottles, measuring cups, wire whisks, and wooden spoons do you own? How many plates do you have compared to the people living in your space? Do you have an ordinary set and a fancy set you never use? How many forks and knives? Do you have more than one garlic press, vase for flowers, pots, pans? You may need more than one of some of the things you own, but be honest about the things you have too many of. If you get stuck on this one—say, you aren't sure if you need more than one grapefruit sectioning tool or not— explore this. After (*not* during) the home release, try a "just one" experiment. Make a little collection of the things you are questioning and put it in one place. You might include one coffee cup, one plate, one fork, one pen, and one pair of sunglasses, or whatever else you have several of. For a few weeks, use only the items from your kit and see how it feels. See if using fewer items than usual adds to your stress or reduces it.

Then, what about the passed-down items that you never use, like your grandmother's china or that fifty-cup coffeemaker? How about the punch bowl? Next, look at the consumables, food, spices, vitamins, and so on in your cabinets, drawers, fridge, and freezer. What is in the way of you enjoying the good stuff? Spices are a great example of this. There are probably only three to five spices you use on a regular basis and maybe seven to twelve you use often. If you collect spices like I did, you may have twenty to fifty sitting in your cabinet. Which might mean you have so many that you can't find the ones you enjoy. This goes for the pantry items, too. When they build up, it doesn't only make the ones you are looking for harder to find; it also makes going into that cabinet less appealing overall. Who looks forward to making dinner when it's impossible to find what you need?

Bathrooms: Separate toiletries, cosmetics, and skin care into opened and unopened. Designate any unopened containers to be donated to a local shelter. For everything already opened, do a quick, ruthless sort. Pile one: "I use this." Pile two: "I do not use this." Then do one last sort through pile one, separating items into "I like using this" and "I do not like using this." Next look at your towels and other linens. If you have more than two sets per person, is that necessary? Would one be enough? Have you ever used the third set? When it comes to cosmetics and skin care, consider simplifying your daily routine. Pick two or three items that do the most and hide the rest for thirty days. Remember: If you don't miss it, release it. Do you really have time for a ten-step skin care routine? Same goes for makeup. What do you actually wear? Keep that and let the rest go.

Living Room: Start with media. If you watch all shows and movies with streaming, do you need those discs, cassette tapes, and other outdated media? I'm not answering this for you. It's different for everyone. I got rid of all of mine except for a handful of holiday movies (yes, I kept *The Holiday*), and I am also keeping (and not apologizing for) my *Gilmore Girls* DVD box set. Like I said, it's different for everyone. Next, release the décor. You know, the vases, frames, and other Pottery Barn–esque items you bought to make it look nice, but you only notice them when you dust them. Less stuff = less cleaning. Finally, after releasing any other items you never use, why not let go of some of that furniture if you don't want it anymore? I remember when we had a living room and a family room. We filled them both with furniture, art, curtains, the works. We spent most of our time in one room over the other, so we let go of everything in the second room. That was when we knew we had too much house.

Garage/shed/attic: Hidden stuff is still stuff. Sometimes we put things in these spaces because we think we'll use it later, then we forget we have it at all and either repurchase it or realize we don't need it anymore. I wish I could share pictures of my garage and shed from my first house with you, if only to show you that you don't have to feel bad for saving things you know you will never use. I'm trying to remember what I kept in those always-full spaces. There were items I hadn't used for years that lived in boxes because I thought I was supposed to keep them forever. Until I began to equate stuff with stress, I just carried those things with me whenever I moved, finding a new hidden storage space for them. Then they got too heavy. Sometimes when something gets too heavy, we buy storage space and put it there. Since you'll eventually let it go anyway, save the expense, recognize that it has served its purpose, and let it go.

Bedroom: Clean out your nightstands, check the top of your dresser. Is it clear of clutter, or does it seem like you have a bedroom full of things that have nowhere else to live? If you have extra furniture in your bedroom, do you use it or is it just extra counter space? Chairdrobe, anyone? The most important thing you do in your bedroom is sleep. Remove anything that disturbs your sleep. If you are wondering, "What about my partner?" I am going to leave that up to you.

Kids' Bedrooms: If your kids are old enough, talk to them about decluttering. If they aren't, limit their things but make it fun. This should not feel like a punishment for kids. Most of that stuff in their bedrooms wasn't their idea or their decision. You might discover that, like you, they have their favorite things, too, and would enjoy more space for them. If they are less distracted, it's likely that they'll be more engaged. I remember reading books to my daughter before she fell asleep; even though she had several options, we'd always choose the same favorites again and again. *Goodnight Moon.*

Closets: Remove anything that doesn't fit today and anything that makes you feel bad when you wear it or don't wear it. Then take out the items with tags still hanging, the stuff you are only keeping because it was soooo cheap or because it was verrrry expensive. These are not good reasons to buy items or to keep them. Next, let go of the duplicates and the gifts if you don't wear them. If there are clothes in there you bought for a life or a job you don't have anymore, say goodbye to those items without regret. Once you've let go of most of the clothes in your closet, ask yourself if you love getting dressed with fewer items. If so, try my Project 333 challenge.[1] People say that it is life-changing. It was for me.

Junk drawers/cabinets/rooms: These are the spaces where you put things because you don't know what they do, what they belong to, or where they go. These things on their own are signs that they don't need to stay in your home anymore. We could add cords and chargers into this category, too. If you have a box of cords and don't know what they do, welcome to being an adult in the digital age. Set aside some time to figure out what they do; let go of the ones you don't need anymore (which will probably be most of them).

Office: Gather the paper. Make a pile of papers that require action in the next thirty days. This may include bills that need to be paid, appointments that need to be made, or anything else that requires more immediate action. Make a second pile of all other papers. You aren't filing, sorting, labeling, or shredding. You're just gathering. Clean off the desk or work surface. Only keep what you use. Once you get through the decluttering, I recommend limiting the amount of "organizing" you do. If you only have a small pile of papers left, they can probably all go together or live in two folders or piles, which you can then label "action" and "archive." The action folder holds those items that require action in the near future, and the archive folder holds the rest. You may have to sort through a few papers to find what you are looking for in the archive file, but the amount of times you actually need something compared to the time you might spend thoughtfully organizing all of it? Again, bad life math.

Home release release strategy: This might be the most important part of the home release. If you've moved through all the spaces in your home and filled bags and boxes, now it's time to physically get it out of your home, your car, and your life. This is often the time we just scooch a bag into a corner or a box into the closet or under the bed. How long have bags of clothes to donate lived in the trunk of your car? If you can move the things from your home release to their new home immediately, you will feel the weight lifting. More important, you'll be creating space instead of just shifting stuff around.

In thirty days, do the whole process again. That will give you time to see how you feel about the work you did during the first round of your home release. If you can barely remember what you got rid of or you are really enjoying this new space, you'll feel more confident to let go of even more. You may notice you don't need a bigger closet or house. Maybe you'll even start to think this would be a good time to downsize (that's what happened to me). Subsequent rounds of home release may be harder in the sense that you have less to let go of, and you may be moving on to things that feel harder to release. In other ways, though, it will be easier. You'll know what to expect and how to make it more fun.

One last thing to consider if you struggle to let go of your stuff. Decluttering is one part dealing with your stuff and three parts dealing with your heart. This is why letting go is hard. Because stuff isn't just stuff in our hearts. Stuff is the moment someone said hello or goodbye. It's a pair of shoes we never thought we could afford or decades of photos that remind us that we had a life. Stuff is dozens of report cards and yearbooks, and it's also forty-nine coffee cups (even though we always use our favorite one). All of that is true about stuff in our hearts. *And* there is a possibility for fuller lives, less stress, moving with more ease, more clarity about what matters, more time to engage in what you discover matters to you, more presence and connection with the people you love, better sleep, space for creativity, and room to take care of yourself.

And even better news... there is a place in between *all* stuff and *no* stuff that will allow you to not only shift your focus from defining who you are by what you own but also to enjoy your favorite things. It's your simplicity, your home, your life. You make the rules.

Knowing that your heart may be holding on a little too tightly, be gentle with yourself. Go easy; take tiny steps and lots of breaks as you work toward a more spacious, relaxed life.

The Tiny Steps

Your heart really wants tiny steps when it comes to decluttering and letting go.

- ❖ *Create home release questions.* Jot down the questions and conversations you want to have with yourself or with your family before the home release, like the ones under the "Connect with your team" heading on page 85. If you are doing this alone, bounce your ideas off someone you trust or journal through your answers. If you are doing this with others, give them the questions in advance so they can take some time to think about them. This is something you may have been considering for a while, but it's brand-new to them. Don't expect everyone to be as enthusiastic as you are. These conversations will make a difference and contribute to a deeper understanding of why you want to make this change.
- ❖ *Keep a tally of what you use on a day-to-day basis.* Keep a list for a week or so about what you actually use, wear, or enjoy every day. You'll quickly identify your favorites when you see them appear on every list. You may also be surprised with how little you use. While there will be a few seasonal items to consider, for the most part you'll get a good idea of what you don't need anymore.

❖ *Give your emotions some attention.* Letting go brings things up. You may feel sad, nervous, annoyed, and even angry that you spent money on things that mean nothing to you now, or that you are spending a precious Saturday removing things that you spent another precious Saturday shopping for. These are all valid feelings, but none of them indicate that you should continue to hold on to the stuff.

❖ *Do it alone first.* If your family isn't on board, don't insist they join you. Instead, create a modified home release that you can do on your own. Don't focus on their stuff, only yours. You may inspire them with your actions and/or learn some things that will help you all do a future home release together.

One Gentle Step

If the idea of a home release feels like too much, try this One Gentle Step: Set the date for a one-hour home release. Do a mini version and see how much you can get done.

Permission Slip:

My home isn't just a place to keep my stuff. It's a place for love and connection. I will make space for more of that.

TWO

Unbothered

You know that saying, "If it costs you your peace, it's too expensive"? Often, we think that other people and situations are robbing us of our peace and there is very little we can do about it. The truth is that every time we get bothered, we are the ones actively spending away our peace. It could be on the littlest stuff, too; in fact, it usually is. Have you ever been bothered by things like:

- the sound of someone chewing their food?
- the tone of an email?
- the way you think someone is looking at you or thinking about you?

The Gentle You is naturally unbothered by things like the above because she knows that we hold all the power over what will annoy or not annoy us. And she knows that it's best to hold on to our precious peace. Let's recognize that it's within us to decide if we are going to give up even a sliver of our peace over the sound of someone else enjoying their dinner. So how do we do this? In this situation and many others, there are a few good options. For example:

1. Walk away. Say: "Excuse me, I have to take this call / go to the bathroom / say a prayer / jot down a note..." This strategy is perfect with anything that bothers you on the internet, too, and you don't even have to say a word; just turn off your phone or close your computer and walk away. If you walk far enough, you'll forget about that annoying comment, meme, or post entirely.

2. Reframe. When you think, *That is so annoying*, then as soon as you say it to yourself, your brain is like, *Yes, this is* really *annoying.* Instead, you could just as easily send your brain a different signal by saying: *Awww, that's adorable how they are chewing their food without a care in the world. They must be really relaxed.* This is obviously easier for the little things. It's OK if at first you still think, *That is so annoying.* Just chase it with the alternative reframe. Your brain will soon pick up the good habit.

3. Speak up. This doesn't always help, but if you can think of a kind way to say, "Could you not?" then give it a go. If you are already very bothered, though, don't say anything. You likely won't express yourself in a way that the other person can receive. Worst-case scenario, it leads to an argument. Who has the energy to argue about how to eat dinner?

4. Look in the mirror. This may be a good time to recognize that you are probably bothering someone, too. When was the last time you watched yourself chew food? People are annoying, and we are all people. Remembering this makes me laugh and often snaps me out of hyperfocusing on the annoying person next to me. The reality is that I don't give any thought to my own chewing and annoyingness. It could be unpleasant to listen to and I'm not really sure

I want to hear that from someone at this point. I'm all for self-improvement, but come on.

(Note: Every one of these recommendations can be applied to bigger, more significant bothers. It may just take a little finessing.)

Simply becoming aware of how vital our peace is to feeling good and functioning makes it easier to maintain. When we aren't aware, it's harder to be gentle: We spend all our energy trying to change others or being unwilling to accept something that is happening (even though it's happening whether we are bothered or not). Keeping your peace isn't a sign of support for something you don't support. It's not faking your feelings. It's how you move through something more gently. It's how you decide how you want to respond. It's how you protect and nourish the Gentle You.

Notice when you are more easily bothered. Is it when you first wake up? Before coffee? When you are hungry? When you are tired? This is the wrong time to engage in things that may bother you. It's the worst time to check the news, have a difficult conversation, or be around people who tend to annoy you. When you can identify these more challenging times for yourself, you can alleviate stress by steering clear of bothersome things during this time. Of course, you can't always control what might come up, but steering yourself away from bother during these times will help you retain more peace for those unexpected moments because you are going to need it.

Here's something you've heard before: "You can't change other people, you can only change yourself." I know. Very annoying. But it's still true. I have a friend whom I loved (and still love) very much and whom I used to really struggle with. Yes, you can love someone and be bothered by them at the same time. In fact, the people who bother us the most are often the ones we love the most. This friend loved to bother me—or should I say, I allowed myself to be bothered by him. This relationship frustrated me so much that I finally asked my therapist what I could say to change our conversations. How could I phrase for him exactly what I wanted to say so my friend would finally understand? I tried to make my therapist believe I was asking about how to change something within me but she saw right through that little game. She said, "It doesn't matter what you say or how you say it." Until that moment, I thought that, compared to this friend, I was the enlightened one, the one willing to change for the better of the relationship. She made me realize that I was just the one willing to change my delivery in hopes of changing my friend. Damn you, therapy!

In the end, I realized that I had to look at the changes I was willing to make, knowing my friend wasn't going to change just because I wanted him to. I had options. Instead of engaging and responding and fighting and rolling my eyes and all of the other ways I expressed how bothered I was, I just stopped. I prioritized my peace instead. That did not change my friend. Still, I am less bothered because I don't spend an ounce of peace on these issues in our relationship. There is no longer anything to fix or figure out. I now know that if I want to be a part of this friendship—as I want to be—I have to accept it for what it is. In other situations, ending a relationship may be the gentler choice. This time, letting go of what I thought it should be and accepting it for what it was worked best. (Note: If you are my friend and wondering if this is you, probably not. Also: If you are my friend and did this with me for our relationship, thank you.)

When it comes to things like climate change, gun control, and/or other things that are mostly out of your control, you can be less bothered there, too. I am not for a moment suggesting you turn your back on important issues. *How* you care about them is what counts. Sometimes your lack of peace is a false economy. Recognize that your stress and worry isn't changing anything around you, it's only changing things within you. As you get angrier, more worried, more agitated, you are bothered. If you are always bothered, you are always angry, which will lead to you being stressed out and eventually getting sick, exhausted, and/or overwhelmed.

At that point of total burnout, you can't make even a little difference anymore. Staying connected to the Gentle You will allow you to, as Together Rising, one of my favorite advocacy-based nonprofits, puts it, turn your heartbreak into effective action. When you know that it's in the best interest of the situation for you to not be that bothered, you can spot a problem and contribute to a solution, all while holding on to your peace. You don't have to be completely outraged and overwhelmed to make a difference. Let me be clear: In some cases, it can take that spark of outrage for you to realize how much you care and move into action. But once you do, get your hands on your heart or take deep breaths, get off social media or go for a walk (or all of the above), and remember the impact you can make without giving up all of your peace.

So what do you do when you forget to be unbothered? Because you are going to get bothered even though you decided you will not get bothered. Normally you would tell yourself, *I can't believe I got bothered again. I have no self-control! I am so bad at this!* The Gentle You says, *I'm glad I noticed how I got bothered by this, and next time I may be able to move through it more gently.* And that's it. No long-winded suffering about how you messed up, can't do it, and so on. Only noticing and moving forward.

Something will come along that unnerves you, something that has you lose your ever-loving peace. You won't be able to collect yourself until you notice that it's time to protect your peace. The good news is that once you notice, you are usually only one or one hundred deep breaths away from reclaiming your peace. Remember, Gentle isn't pretending that things are perfect or ignoring pain in ourselves or in the world. It's simply moving through with more attention, compassion, and hope.

The Tiny Steps

Becoming unbothered is a big deal, especially if you are right in the middle of being very bothered. Instead of shooting for an overnight transformation, try some tiny steps.

- *Create a temporary exit strategy.* As we've established, many of the bothersome things we deal with are perpetual problems and not solvable problems. The only solution may be to remove yourself. However, when you are in it and very bothered, it's hard to know how to get out. During a time of relative peace, create an exit strategy. Figure out where you can step away to, so you can remove yourself from the situation, get unbothered, and come back. Decide on your script, like "I have to go to the bathroom," or "Oh, I forgot I need to return this call."

- *Make yourself laugh.* Since there may not be a reasonable solution to your bother, distract yourself with laughter. Think back to a funny moment: "Remember that time when we threw our pillows on the front lawn at four in the morning to watch the meteor shower and I thought something was about to get us but it was just the sprinklers across the street?" This just happened, by the way. We did see a fireball and two meteors, but the highlight of this event was me jumping up screaming in the dark for no reason at all. Just thinking about it moved me from being bothered to being amused. Now I'm a little softer.

❖ *Give the botherer a break.* Just this once, could you let it go? Wouldn't that be the gentle choice, especially if it's not something you can change and it's not something harmful? It's a tiny act of kindness for you and whoever is bothering you. (Note: You don't need to tell them about it, either.)

One Gentle Step

If you are too bothered to do the tiny steps, try one gentle step. Jot down something teeny tiny that bothers you, something you might be a little embarrassed to complain about. Now practice with that one tiny thing for a while. Practice walking away or reframing. Once you can automatically choose peace instead of getting bothered, work on something else.

Permission Slip:

If something or someone is really annoying me, I am allowed to move on without being bothered.

THREE

Count Your Spoons

We measure our time in hours and minutes. We measure our money in dollars and cents. How do we measure our energy? What does a unit of our energy look like? It's a resource that matters just as much as time and money in terms of how we navigate life, but we often overlook it or forget that we don't have an endless supply. We may feel like we don't have as much control over this one. Maybe that's true, but this makes thinking about energy even more important; though we can't always control how much energy we have, we can often determine how much energy we expend. It's not a perfect science, but just being more realistic about this resource is going to make a big difference. It may be more challenging to measure energy exactly, but if you want to work at a pace that honors your personal energy availability, it will help to figure this out. You'll be surprised at how much easier it is to move through the day when you aren't overextending yourself.

In the chronic illness world, there is something called the Spoon Theory, wherein you assign a number of spoons (as units of energy) to specific tasks. The Spoon Theory[1] was created by Christine Miserandino to describe to a friend what it's like for a chronically ill person to navigate a day with limited energy. But we could all benefit from moving through our days at what artist and mindfulness educator Jamila Reddy calls "your authentic pace." We all have twenty-four hours in a day, but we don't all have the same amount of energy to live those hours, not the same as one another or the same as ourselves during different stages of life (or even today versus tomorrow). Some days our spoons just don't go as far. Often this is when we think we have to push through so we can be more productive and keep up with the demands of hustle culture and other made-up shit that keeps us running on empty.

Long before hustle culture, #bossbabes, and the waves of social media posts telling us how to get more done (and look good doing it), we were still out there jumping through hoops, climbing ladders, and doing more than our bodies and brains could tolerate, all in the name of more. In my decades of working in commission-based corporate positions, no one ever regaled me with tales of how they had made too much or worked more than enough that day. Instead, the stories I heard were always about never having enough money, time, or energy. Every story had the same words: "busy," "overwhelmed," "more," "never enough," and "happy hour." I ate those words for breakfast, carried them into my day, and then read self-help books so I could learn how to be better and do more and quit crying and meet my potential. None of those books suggested rest, relaxation, or ease. Far from it. Instead they were all, "dig deep," "push hard," "take the bull by the horns and put your nose to the grindstone!"

Because of this toxic personal-development quest, I used to schedule myself to within an inch of a breakdown. I gave my all. I measured who I was by what I got done. Now I make time and space for myself, not to get more done, but to have more time and space to be gentle. Productivity culture is hardwired within us. If you, too, want time and space to daydream, to rest, to heal, and to be gentle, you are going to have to flip the script and reject this idea of more equaling better in your day-to-day life.

If you're reading this book, I'm guessing you want the time and energy to engage in your own life, to notice simple pleasures, and to connect with inner joy. You want to move from being chronically stressed out to savoring your life. You don't need another productivity hack or get-rich-quick scheme; *you need rest*. You don't need another Zoom meeting; you need a *sanctuary full of what soothes you*. You don't need to hear more about what's wrong with you; *you need stories of hope, ease, and love*.

Most of the productivity hacks that trick us into believing we can get even more done have all had the opposite effect. Instead of being more productive, we are tired, sick, and burned-out. We've become apathetic and unsure about what we want because we feel that we aren't doing enough. Here's why: When you are measuring (and are being measured by) how much you get done, it's never enough. You lose yourself to doing more because you forget how you feel, who you are, and what you want.

Chronic illness isn't the only thing that affects our energy. My spoons go further in the morning than the evening. It would take me twice as long to write this paragraph if I tried to write it after dinner instead of after breakfast. Night owls may have more spoons or BSE (big spoon energy) at night. I usually don't have back-to-back days that are equal in energy. My energy, especially when it comes to creative work, ebbs and flows. When I don't recognize an ebb, I end up doing the pushing-through thing, burning my spoons at both ends. It doesn't feel good and it rarely results in good work. When I allow myself to work at my authentic pace, the process is more enjoyable and the end result is much better.

Imagine if corporations encouraged employees to work in a way that felt good to them. Chelsea Fagen, the founder and CEO of the Financial Diet, a platform and company offering real money talk and financial support for women, cut the average work schedule for her employees from five days to four without cutting their pay. In 2021, after she switched from a forty-hour to a thirty-two-hour workweek, she said, "Revenue increased, everyone was happier, and the same work gets done. We also discovered that three days is the minimum for a good weekend."[2]

Whether or not you are dealing with an illness (or another situation that compromises your energy), evaluate what your day looks like and how much you have to give (and how much you *want* to give). Don't just consult your calendar or to-do list—check in with how you want to feel. Just because there is space on your calendar doesn't mean you have to do more. Since we aren't going to measure who we are by what we accomplish anymore, we can really focus on how we feel. What we crave is not to *be* good but to *feel* good—to stop proving ourselves, to lift each other up, and to clear the obstacles to enjoying our lives.

If you are feeling the pressure to work long after your spoons run out, check in and see what books you are reading, what podcasts you are listening to, and what the people around you are talking about. Who are you listening to, and are you on that list? Notice where the pressure is coming from. Is it coming from around you or within you? It may be time to define (or redefine) "enough" more specifically. When it comes to measuring what is or isn't "enough," consider the following mindset shifts:

- **Money.** Understanding your money (no matter how good or grim the situation is) will help you know if you need to earn more, spend less, and how much to save instead of just assuming that you always need more. For a major change in perspective about what constitutes enough money, I recommend *Your Money or Your Life* by Vicki Robin and Joe Dominguez.

- **Time.** Productivity tips and tricks make us believe that we can squeeze more in, but why should we? I prefer to give my best instead of my most. That means giving less of myself overall. When you are struggling with the pull to do more, when you think, *I have to do . . .*, pause and ask yourself this very simple question: *Do I?* Instead of replacing the discomfort you feel about having free time with more work, question that urge. Notice how you talk about time. "I'm behind." "I have to catch up." Do you have a time scarcity mindset? If so, the solution is to be more present. Maybe the opposite of being all caught up isn't being behind but being relaxed. Where you are right now is where you are. You aren't behind. You aren't caught up. You are here. It's really all you get.

- **Stuff.** Often we are working more to make more money to have more stuff that we don't really want. Once you've gone through a home release or two, you'll notice that you don't want more stuff. You want more life.

The Tiny Steps

These tiny steps will help you identify your spoon-to-spend ratio when it comes to your energy. Protect this valuable resource.

- ☆ *Give 10 percent less.* If you give 100 percent at work, it's unlikely anyone will notice if you start giving only 90 percent. This isn't exact math, but play around with giving a little bit less in different areas of your life. You don't owe 100 percent to your job. That extra 10 percent may be the difference between you running out of spoons or not.

÷ *Cancel a bunch of shit.* Do this one right now. Grab your calendar and clear a whole day or a whole week. You deserve a minute to come back to the Gentle You, and that's harder when you are bouncing from appointment, to meeting, to a game for the kids, to returning calls, emails, text messages, and so on. It's just too much. Don't give too many spoons away. This way, when you need energy for the things that really matter, you'll have more than enough. If unavoidable responsibilities mean that clearing a whole day is impossible, try clearing an hour. Protect your spoons at all costs. Make sure they stay just for you.

÷ *Charge your battery.* We usually charge our phones and refill our gas tanks before they are empty. So why is it OK to let your personal battery run out before you think you deserve to recharge? Instead of waiting until you are sick or exhausted, find ways to recharge throughout the day. Little boosts will keep you going longer than trying to recover from total burnout and an empty tank. This could look like turning off your phone for ten minutes and creating some silence for yourself, or pausing your day to eat lunch instead of eating on the run.

One Gentle Step

If you are running low on spoons and don't want to spend them on the tiny steps, try one gentle step. Simply be curious about your authentic pace. How far away are you from it—and how might you start coming back to it? Is there a new energy-saving routine you want to try, or are there certain times you know you need to reserve for rest? Honor that.

Permission Slip:

I will not give away all of my spoons.

FOUR

Decide What Not to Do

W e are so consumed with the things we need to do that we often discount the power of considering what we are not going to do anymore. This gentle practice is making a "not-to-do" list. Now that you are rethinking how you measure your worth— not measuring who you are by what you do or by how many check marks are on your to-do list—it's the perfect time to work on your not-to-do lists. I like to make a not-to-do list every week or two as a reminder that I am living intentionally and in alignment with what is most important to me. This list doesn't just include what I do, but what I don't do, too. It serves as a reminder when I'm falling into old patterns.

Not-to-dos may involve actual tasks that you'd like other people to do. For instance, in my business it took me a long time to let go of tasks other people could do and tasks other people did better than me. In the beginning, because I didn't have a team, I did it all. Then, even when I didn't have to do it all, I'd make an excuse like, "It will only take a second." It took some time to see that even though I *could* do a certain task, that didn't mean I was the best person to do it.

Other not-to-do lists may focus less on tasks and more on mindset or habits. What do you do just because you've always done it or because you think you are supposed to do it? It may help to have a not-to-do list so you don't autopilot back to your daily go-to easy behavior (the things we use to mitigate baseline stress and exhaustion), like checking email or social media, or getting decimated by the news before even getting out of bed. Below are a few of my not-to-do lists. Writing these out for myself is a gentle reminder that I can choose differently. Most things on these lists used to be automatic. I was doing them without thinking about them at all. In fact, I did them without thinking for decades, and they don't go away overnight. It's a day-by-day process to make or review the list and remember that these actions hurt me. In the spirit of being gentle, I will not knowingly do things that hurt me anymore.

Here are a few examples of my not-to-do lists:

Not-to-do list:
Things I usually don't know I'm doing until it's too late

- Rush.
- Take myself too seriously.
- Compare.
- Say yes to something happening later that I wouldn't say yes to if it was happening right now.
- Push through.
- Ignore what I know is best for me.
- Believe everything I think.

Not to do list: Protect your peace edition
- Overdo it.
- Overthink it.
- Overexplain it.
- Overreact to it.

Not-to-do list: The needless worry list
- Assume what anyone is thinking.
- Worry about things outside of my control.
- Scroll.
- Compromise my sleep.

Not-to-do list: Mornings
- Snooze button.
- Email.
- Social media.
- News.

Whenever I make a not-to-do list, I always spend a few hours (or even a few days) feeling hyperaware of the actions on the list. I don't magically stop doing these things instantly and forever. However, after the same thing appears on multiple lists, it starts to sink in. I don't know how long it took but now, even without a list, I don't check the news at the beginning or end of the day anymore. That's just one instance of how something I practiced not doing eventually took hold.

Creating these lists will help you be more mindful about how you aren't spending your time. This creates more time for things you want to do. As I mentioned, this won't magically change all your habits. You may notice yourself doing something on your not-to-do list. It's part of the process, so if that's happening, don't think you aren't doing it perfectly, but celebrate that you are doing it right. Not-to-do lists may also inspire you to do nothing at all.

My not-to-do lists helped me to stop expecting certain things to happen at certain times. Once I was open to the thought of removing imaginary timelines and deadlines, being less hurried and more gentle, the idea of slowing down and taking things as they come started showing up in conversations and in my Instagram feed. Isn't that how it always happens? We say that "the stars align," but what really happens is that we align. We get into alignment with exactly what we want and need in our lives when we quiet some of the noise around us (and within us) and start tapping into what our insides have been asking for. This quest for something more gentle wasn't anything new for my insides. For years, my heart and nervous system had been softly asking me for something different. I ignored those pleas as long as I could because I didn't think I was allowed to thrive in my life without pushing and doing more and more and more to be better and better and better. It. Was. Never. Enough. Perhaps as you read these words, you are noticing that you are perfectly aligned to the idea of finally being gentle, too.

Once I was aligned on the inside, I was able to reset my own internal algorithm so I could more easily filter out the messages that tried to enforce "never enough"—they just didn't resonate with me anymore. As author and therapist Lisa Olivera says, "My intuition is my algorithm." We are so used to aligning with the outside algorithms of our Instagram feed, Google searches, and the people in our lives who really want us to adopt what's best for them. Instead, let your intuition be your algorithm. Pay attention to the signs and stars you are aligning with. This is how you begin to trust yourself, to trust the Gentle You. When your phone or computer freezes up, instead of forcing it back to life, put it down. Put your hands on your heart, take a walk, or lie down in the middle of the day. When you are ready, the Gentle You is listening and preparing the messages and reinforcement you desire.

The Tiny Steps

These tiny steps will help you create your not-to-do lists and use them to better align with what you want in life.

- *Theme your lists.* Name a few of the not-to-do lists you'd like to create. For instance, a morning not-to-do, phone not-to-do, relationship not-to-do, or protect-your-peace not-to-do list. By creating a theme for your not-to-do list, you can focus on one area that may be taking more of your time, energy, or peace.

- *Put it front and center.* Make phone wallpaper out of your not-to-do list. Then, before you scroll social media, you may see that comparing your insides to other people's outsides is at the top of your not-to-do list, and you'll skip the social check-in (or do it more mindfully). These not-to-do lists are helping you break habits that aren't working in your favor, but it's hard to remember what you don't want to do if they're actions you do without much thought. Sticky notes and other reminders will help you stay on track.

- *Switch it up:* Make a new not-to-do list each week so you can see what works best for you. You aren't creating life-long rules but simply drawing your attention to the power you have when it comes to how you spend your time and energy.

One Gentle Step

If the tiny steps are on your first not-to-do list, try this one gentle step. Instead of committing to weekly lists, identify one thing you don't want to do today. Just one.

Permission Slip:

What I choose not to do is just as important as what I choose to do.

FIVE

Less Phone

One morning, my husband and I decided to try something new on our early-morning hike. Where I live in Salt Lake City, we're surrounded by mountains, so we often go hiking, especially on summer mornings before the heat rolls in. I usually take a bunch of pictures and videos as we move through the mountains. Later I share them in an Instagram Story series called "Today's Walk." I love sharing the wildflowers, vistas, and pictures of moose, deer, and other wildlife we come across. We have undoubtedly some of the most beautiful surroundings in the country. We're lucky—mountain lakes or mama moose with their babes in our own backyard is not something everyone gets to experience.

On a hike the week before, my husband had made an interesting suggestion. He said, "Next time we hike, let's turn off our phones." He was forty days into a social media break (which would eventually become permanent). I loved the idea. Even though sharing pictures from our hikes was something I enjoyed, I knew seeing things through the camera lens was different from really seeing them. Not better or worse . . . just different. Even though I had taken plenty of phone breaks, turned off notifications, and set boundaries around social media, I never thought about my photography habit as something to experiment with. After all, I often referred to this device as "my camera that has internet and a phone." When he suggested not even using that part of it, I noticed a resistance bubbling up. It reminded me that I probably had something to learn here. So for this hike, as we get ready, I lace up my boots, then turn my phone off and tuck it away in my bag. As soon as I see the bright pops of color from the blooming wildflowers, I think, *I have to capture this.* Then I remember that I am not using my phone on this hike. I think about all of the other pictures of wildflowers I have. Do I need more?

After that moment, I turn my attention away from my phone to really take in my surroundings. Not only am I more present for the jaw-dropping scenery; I'm also more tuned in to conversations along the way. There is nothing to distract me or remove me. And as a bonus, I don't get consumed by a few text messages because I looked at my phone to take a picture. We find a spot by the lake and take out our picnic breakfast (iced coffee included). There isn't a photo shoot of our beautiful spread, but I can still remember the sound of the ice clinking on the glasses and how the sun shimmered on the lake. Even though I didn't use my phone that day (and I left my Fitbit at home), the hike counted. The picnic mattered. Even though there are no photos to prove it, that day still happened.

When I used to think about how my phone pulls me out of my life, I'd think about things like notifications and social media scrolling. I wasn't thinking about taking pictures on my hikes and how I was limiting myself from taking in my surroundings. Now, I still use my phone and take pictures on some of our hikes, but because I know the difference between what it feels like with more phone and with less phone, I can choose more intentionally.

One January, I hosted a "Less Phone, More Life" challenge online (I know, ironic). My promise was to help people reduce their screen time by 25 percent after our week together. It worked! By implementing one tiny change every day for a few days, most people who participated in the group found their screen time dropped without having to exercise willpower or locking their phones up. I'll share some of these powerful strategies below.

As a writer, I knew I didn't need a visual recording to share my hikes. I could tell a story. I could describe the scene. I could bring people in with my words. Or, I could save some of it just for myself. We don't have to share it all. We are allowed to fully experience something without posting on socials or sending pictures to friends and family. When we do, we're more likely to actually be in the moment, feel it, enjoy it, and remember it. Once again, less becomes so much more.

I'm not asking you to get rid of your device. Our phones are here to stay. This means that modifying them to be less appealing is an important step in spending less time on our phones and more time in our lives. The following adjustments will also help you see where your phone is really adding value to your life and when it's simply distracting you from what's right in front of you. There's nothing to lose by giving a few of these a try, especially when compared to the things you may gain. When you spend less time on your phone, you'll enjoy more free time, a better attention span, and more human connection.

1. REMOVE EMAIL FROM YOUR PHONE

I removed email from my phone a long time ago and don't miss it at all. Over several years, there have been less than a handful

of times when I've felt email on my phone could have been helpful. By never looking at email on my phone, I've reclaimed time
and mental space. If you notice you check email on your phone
but don't take any action (or don't take meaningful action) like
replying or forwarding or anything else those emails require, it's
a waste of your time (and makes it more likely you'll forget to do
those actions later!). Instead of chipping away at your email all day
long, save it until you are back at your desk or computer, or carve
out time specifically for handling email. If you aren't sure if this
will work for you, experiment. Try thirty days without email on
your phone and see how it feels.

2. DON'T KEEP APPS ON THE HOME SCREEN
OR IN NEATLY LABELED CONTAINERS

Instead, keep all apps in one folder. I open an app by typing the
app name in the search bar. That way I'm not tempted to open
an app just because I see it on my phone when I'm innocently
checking the time or the weather. For the most part, you'll likely
forget the other apps are there at all. Don't worry, you'll still be
able to keep all of your apps; they just won't be the center of attention anymore. You know when you open your phone and see all
your apps vying for your attention? Those times you didn't even
know you wanted to open Instagram, but now you're deep into a
scroll? That's because app icons are designed to be eye-catching and
appealing to the human eye. They want us to click on them! Without seeing your apps when you open your phone, you'll be more
intentional about how you want to spend time on your phone, if
at all. If you want to take it to the next level, why not delete social
media apps? You can catch up on your desktop or download them

again if you want to post something from your phone. Sometimes an empty home screen will remind you to look up.

3. TURN OFF ALL NOTIFICATIONS EXCEPT FOR PHONE OR TEXT

Turn off social notifications, news updates, useless reminders that apps send you to keep you engaged, and anything else that feels more distracting than helpful. Studies show that it takes an average of twenty-three minutes to bounce back from a distraction. Stay more focused with notifications off. If your calendar notifications are helpful, keep them on. Otherwise turn them off, too.

4. BE HONEST ABOUT HOW MUCH TIME YOU SPEND ON YOUR PHONE

If you are concerned with your phone usage, notice when, how, and why you use your phone, particularly certain apps. If you want to find out where most of your phone time goes, try an app like Moment. Or, for a quick glance of your mobile minutes and how long you're spending on each app, search "battery" in your settings. There should be an option to show activity by time or percentage.

5. DO NOT DISTURB

There is a Do Not Disturb feature on your phone for a reason. As well as switching it on and off manually, you can set it to come on at certain times. Mine is set from 7:00 p.m. to 7:00 a.m., and I switch it on when I'm working on projects. Airplane mode or turn-ing your phone off works, too, but when you use the Do Not Dis-turb feature, you can set it up so your "favorites" can still contact you. If there is an emergency, my closest people can get through, but no one else can.

6. GO GRAY

Make your phone less appealing to look at by changing the set-tings to grayscale. As technology is always changing, check the lat-est specifications on your phone model.

7. SLOW THE SCROLL

If you find yourself mindlessly scrolling, put an elastic band or hair tie around the middle of your phone. Even a sticky note in the center of your phone will help you pause. Adding a little friction between you and your phone gives you enough time to consider how you really want to spend your time.

8. IF YOU WANT TO SPEND LESS TIME ON YOUR PHONE, WELCOME BOREDOM

One of the biggest problems of being on our phones all the time is that we don't get bored. Some of my most creative moments have come from boredom. Make time to get bored and check in with yourself. When you have nothing to do, just sit there instead of picking up your phone. Look around at all of the other sources of wisdom and inspiration in your life before you scroll through Insta-gram, especially the one within.

9. STOP FILLING ALL THE SPACES

We love to check our phones when we are waiting in line, waiting for an appointment, or in between work tasks. The next time you're at a stoplight, look to your left and right; chances are, you'll spot a driver checking their phone. We're filling all the spaces instead of enjoying them, instead of letting them unfold, and instead of being alone with our own thoughts. See what happens when you stop filling all the spaces. Next time you're waiting for someone or something, just...wait. The world is noisy enough. Let some of it be quiet.

10. FOLLOW FEWER PEOPLE TO SPEND LESS TIME ON YOUR PHONE

If you spend most of your time on social media apps, unfollow as many people as possible. As an experiment years ago, I unfollowed everyone on Twitter with the intention of coming back more thoughtfully. Instead, I kind of forgot to go back. After a month experimenting with no TikTok, I realized I didn't miss it. I think TikTok creators are wonderfully creative and entertaining, but watching them was filling all of *my* creative spaces.

11. BE TOGETHER, TOGETHER

Even though it seems like you are spending time with the people you love, look around. Are you all spending time on your phones instead? Being alone, together? Instead, create outings, activities, and opportunities to be together, together without screens.

12. FIND SOMETHING THAT MATTERS MORE

Share a picture on your lock screen of something or someone that matters more than what's on the other side. Sometimes we just need that reminder that what's happening around us is better than what we think we are going to find on our phones.

The Tiny Steps

These tiny steps will help you determine what enough means to you when it comes to spending time on your phone. Try them for a week or two and see if they help you reduce your screen time by 25 percent.

- *Make a "what matters more" list.* When it comes to relieving boredom, your phone is the path of least resistance. Don't force yourself to figure out another solution on the spot. Instead, keep a short list of things you'd rather do. Try not to keep this list on your phone. Even if you have only one thing on the list, it will still prevent you from going to your phone first. For instance, I always keep a book nearby. Instead of opening my phone first, I open the book and read at least a couple of sentences.
- *Leave your phone at home.* Our next gentle practice is going to help more with this, but for now: The easiest way to stay off your phone is to stay away from your phone.
- *Identify screen-free zones* (times and places). This is your chance to cultivate distraction-free places to enjoy more of your real life. Maybe it's first thing in the morning or just before bed. Maybe at the dinner table, in the bathroom, or while driving your car. Creating these zones will keep you off your screens.

One Gentle Step

If you want to skip the tiny steps for now, try this one gentle step. Instead of phone-first mornings, put your hands on your heart before you put them on your phone. Each morning, before you check the weather, see what's going on in your email, or look at an adorable puppy picture on Instagram, just wait. Check in with yourself first.

Permission Slip:

I can leave my phone at home sometimes and enjoy less phone and more life.

SIX

Unplug

Maybe I should have named this chapter "Way Less Phone." Instead of having you just take little breaks or turn your notifications off, this gentle practice is going to invite you to take at least twenty-four hours away from your digital devices every week. I've been a fan of longer breaks from the internet for a while, but it wasn't until I read Tiffany Shlain's book *24/6: Giving Up Screens One Day a Week to Get More Time, Creativity and Connection*[1] that I knew I was focusing on the wrong thing. I was so wrapped up in the digital break part that I didn't consider how to spend the "more time, creativity, and connection." For more than ten years, Tiffany and her family have been having weekly Tech Shabbats. Some of Shlain's recommendations for a successful Tech Shabbat include getting a landline, carrying a notepad, or using a record player. The recommendation that was most interesting to me, the one that really helped me look at digital breaks differently, was this one: Add a tradition. "The idea is to have something extra and unique," Shlain says. Her family kicks off Tech Shabbat by making challah and sharing a big meal.

Your tradition can be absolutely anything that marks the day as different. A long morning walk, an afternoon of board games, or a bedtime dance party. When we take a break from the internet, we are less distracted, more in our lives, able to be present for ourselves, our loved ones, and our interests, and time flows more slowly. Every time I take twenty-four hours off the internet, I feel a little antsy for the first few hours. Even though I really have nothing to check, my brain is used to looking at my phone and it wonders what we are missing. But by the point that it's time to plug back in, I'm not in a hurry to come back. Never have I returned to anyone wondering where I was. Never have I had to work harder to catch up. The internet was just fine without me, and there is no doubt that I was better without it.

These stats may inspire you to give unplugging for twenty-four hours a try. According to an extensive, fact-checked 2023 survey by Zippia.com,[2] the average American checks their phone ninety-six times per day, or once every ten to twelve minutes. The number of times we actually touch our phones is even higher: up to 2,617 times per day. The elastic band, hair tie, or sticky notes I mentioned in the last chapter will provide enough of a pause that it might stop you from looking at your phone altogether. I've also been experimenting with an app called one sec that insists on a one-second pause before opening another app like Instagram. You'd be surprised how long one second is when you are going in for a quick check.

If you think a whole day away from the internet might help you get in touch with the Gentle You, but you are worried about family emergencies, tell your family what to expect. If you do have a landline, ask them to call you there in the event of an emergency. Or, if you want certain family members to be able to reach you anytime, ask them not to text or email but to call you. Then, set up Do Not Disturb on your phone with the very few people who are an exception. If you feel nervous because you usually reply to email immediately, set up a friendly auto-response and let people know when you'll get back to them. Most of these fears are unrealized, but having a back-up plan will help you enjoy your time off.

The Tiny Steps

If you are ready to consider a twenty-four-hour tech break, these tiny steps will help you get ready.

- *Consider your tradition.* How do you want to spend your offline time? Do you want to bake bread, invite friends over, or create a lovely evening of reading and skin care? You can't do this wrong, so check in with yourself. Maybe you'll think back to how you spent your time pre-internet, use this time to start a new hobby, or simply leave the time open.
- *Create your own rules.* If you enjoy listening to music but don't want to buy a record player, you may decide to create a playlist just for your break. If responding to a family member via text or phone is nonnegotiable, build it in but create boundaries like who you'll immediately respond to and what you'll say to keep the conversation short. Do what you need to do so that responding to a text doesn't lead to other digital activity. In other words, don't throw away the whole challenge because one small part doesn't work for you.
- *Reach out.* If you're worried about certain people finding you when you are taking your digital break, get in touch with them first. Let them know how best to reach out. For anyone who can wait, ask them to please wait.

÷ *Schedule your break.* Choose a specific twenty-four-hour period, like 7:00 p.m. on Friday evening to 7:00 p.m. on Saturday. Then put it on your calendar so you can prepare. Try to anticipate what you'll need to find on the internet during this period, then access it in advance and print it out if necessary.

÷ *Evaluate.* After your break, notice what happened. Did time move more slowly? Did you have more time for what you are interested in? Were there any downsides? If friends or family did this with you, ask them, too. What would have made your digital break even better?

One Gentle Step

If you are feeling too nervous or aren't quite ready for the tiny steps that will get you ready to unplug for twenty-four hours, try this one gentle step.

Assign a spot in your home for your digital devices that is tucked away, like a drawer, a closet, or even a locked box. Keeping your devices out of sight will help you fight the temptation for a quick check-in.

Permission Slip:

The internet will be OK without me, and I'll be better off without the internet (for at least twenty-four hours).

SEVEN

Drink Less

I started drinking when I was a teenager and didn't stop until early 2019. As an adult, I mostly managed alcohol well except for a few times a year, often when traveling or getting together with friends or family. I enjoyed drinking, and occasionally I had way too much alcohol, but I wasn't ever addicted to it. I could easily quit drinking for a month or more at a time. I kept coming back, though. I wanted to hold on to those facts I'd heard about how one glass of wine a day is good for you, but honestly, how often did I ever have just one glass? The older I got the harder drinking became. Just a glass or two affected my sleeping and made me feel crappy the following day. I noticed it affected my moods more, too.

In 2011, I wrote a blog post about my concerns about alcohol, and I came to the conclusion that it was fine because I wasn't addicted, didn't have a problem, and wasn't an alcoholic. If I could go back and send a message to the me who wrote those words and thought those thoughts, the Gentle Me would have asked her, "Is not having a label a good enough reason to keep drinking?" and "Is alcohol contributing to the full, healthy, intentional life you say you want? Is it an essential piece of the life you actually want?"

I never intended to stop drinking completely. In January 2019, I woke up with a major hangover. I was on a family getaway to Austin, Texas, and we'd just had a fun night of dinner, dancing, and, yes, drinking. My head was pounding, my mouth was dry, and I could not think clearly. That night, when I started to feel a little better, I decided to take a break from drinking alcohol. I thought it would be a thirty-day break. Then I decided to stretch it to one hundred days. Then a year. At some point, I forgot to miss alcohol. I realized that if I felt better during alcohol breaks, maybe I should make it permanent.

My life is better without alcohol. That's what I usually tell people when they ask me why I don't drink. This gentle practice might be polarizing, and I understand why. You may not drink at all and want to skip this practice altogether. You may question your drinking and be nervous and curious to read further, or maybe you are already thinking defensively: "I enjoy a glass of wine with dinner, beer on the weekend, a drink or two at happy hour, celebrating with a champagne toast [or however you like to imbibe]." Because of that you may feel a little challenged or annoyed that I'm suggesting you take a closer look.

The reason I understand is that I've gone through all these stages of alcohol management. I'm not in recovery. I don't call myself an alcoholic, and I never hit any form of rock-bottom (although I did make plenty of questionable choices while drinking). Being alcohol-free doesn't solve all of my problems but, like simplifying my life, it's given me more capacity and clarity to work through those problems. Who knew that after getting rid of most of my stuff, becoming debt-free, downsizing, and leaving a job that wore me out, the thing that would simplify my life the most would be quitting alcohol?

Ten ways not drinking made my life better

1. **I never had a hangover again.**

   When I was drinking alcohol, I would google things like "hangover remedy," "what should I drink to avoid a hangover," and other similar phrases. I hated waking up with a headache, fuzzy brain, and cravings for fast food. As it turns out, if you don't want to be hungover, not drinking alcohol works every time. It seemed like the older I got, the more easily I ended up with a hangover. Even one or two glasses of wine made me feel crappy the next day. I love knowing that I can wake up feeling well anytime.

2. **I saved lots of money.**

   I didn't often drink the cheap stuff, so dinners out were twice as expensive, holidays and vacation drinking were pricey, and even when I wasn't drinking much, I just spent a lot on alcohol. Since I don't have to buy wine or other alcohol for any reason, I've saved money. This was a very cool, unexpected outcome.

3. **I make fewer decisions.**

   Surprisingly, this is one of the things I love most about not drinking alcohol. I never again have to decide what to drink, when to drink, or how much to drink. I don't have to wonder if I'm drinking the right thing, drinking too much, nor do I have to waste energy searching for hangover cures, cocktail recipes, or which wine goes with seafood. In fact, the only time decisions pop up about alcohol or drinking is when I am deciding what to share or write about.

4. **I sleep so much better.**

   Ahhhh sleep. Even a little bit of alcohol interrupted my sleep, and I want all the sleep I can get. Even though I didn't struggle with insomnia, alcohol caused restlessness and fatigue. In her *New York Times* article[1] on the subject, Amelia Nierenberg explains how alcohol can get in the way of a good night of sleep. "A night of drinking can 'fragment,' or interrupt" the normal phases of deeper and lighter sleep we go through every night, "and you may wake up several times as you ricochet through the usual stages of sleep."[2] "You pay for it in the second half of the night," says Dr. Jennifer Martin, a psychologist and professor of medicine at the University of California, Los Angeles. She goes on to explain that alcohol is "initially sedating, but as it's metabolized, it's very activating." Sleep is so important to me that I'm grateful it's no longer being interrupted by alcohol.

5. **I get to be myself all the time.**

   I'm an introvert but drinking made me feel much more social and outgoing. But when I was drinking, I really wasn't myself, which made me feel bad later. At first I was worried that I wouldn't have as much fun without alcohol. What I've found is that now, I have even more fun because I am spending time with people doing things I actually enjoy. Even though I was more sociable and chatty when I was drinking, without alcohol I'm more confident in who I am. I trust myself more.

6. **Zero regrets after a night out.**

   I never wake up and think, *What happened?* or *What did I say or do?* I never feel bad for drinking too much, staying up too late, or anything else I did when I was drinking. Simply not acting like myself caused regret. Now, when I say or do something out of character, I know I'm probably tired, hungry, or stressed. Without alcohol I can pay attention to what my body is telling me instead of shutting it down with a drink.

7. **I have more clarity and better memory recall.**

Alcohol makes things fuzzy, and not just when you are drinking. I think it affected me more than I realized at the time. There is plenty of data out there on how alcohol affects memory. One study, by Duke University Medical Center, shows that "alcohol can have a dramatic impact on memory. Alcohol primarily disrupts the ability to form new long-term memories...[this] include[s] disruption of activity in the hippocampus, a brain region that plays a central role in the formation of new autobiographical memories."[3]

8. **My life is simpler.**

Decluttering simplified my home; when I quit drinking, I simplified my mental and physical health along with many other parts of my life. I didn't do it for a simple life. I did it for a happier, healthier, more present life. Because I had simplified so many other things before I stopped drinking, I didn't expect to notice a big difference. I did, though. My life is simpler, calmer, and more peaceful without alcohol.

9. **Less risk for multiple health issues.**

Not drinking alcohol lowers my risk of cancer, cardiovascular issues, high blood pressure, depression, memory loss, and other neurological issues. Recommendations in the past have included drinking healthy levels of alcohol but now, based on current data, the American Cancer Society says there are no safe levels. It recommends not drinking alcohol at all. When I was drinking, I loved to cite studies that showed how drinking a glass or two of wine was healthy, so when the new data said otherwise, I had to pay attention. Not having to pretend to be a medical expert is not the reason why I stopped drinking, but it is a very cool benefit.

10. **I get to show up for my life.**
This may be the one I'm most grateful for. I get to choose presence anytime I want. I am here . . . for all of it. I never have to worry that I can't drive, can't pay attention, or can't make decisions (for myself or my loves). I really love being all the way here for my life, even when it's hard.

I don't share all this because I think everyone should quit drinking. I share it to encourage anyone who is tired of hangovers, regrets, and alcohol-related drama and decisions.

Before I stopped for good, I didn't think alcohol was a problem for me. I didn't think I was an alcoholic. I didn't think I needed to quit drinking, but eventually *I wanted to.* For the longest time, I thought drinking was fun and relaxing. Now that it's been out of my life for many years, it's clear that the fun and relaxation usually lasted a moment but then often turned into not feeling well physically and mentally—the opposite of fun and relaxing. In *We Are the Luckiest: The Surprising Magic of a Sober Life*, author Laura McKowen says,[4] "It doesn't matter if you haven't edged as close to disaster as I did. It doesn't matter if no one believes you when you say you have a problem. As they say, it doesn't matter how much you drink, or how often, but what happens to you when you do. If something is keeping you from being fully present and showing up in your life the way you want, then deciding to change that thing is an actual matter of life and death, you know? It's the difference between existing and actually living."

I choose actually living. Fully living. Usually the answer for me is less but when it comes to alcohol, the magic number is none. You may be wondering if I think being sober would simplify your life. I have no idea. It depends on how alcohol affects your life now. I could say the same thing about clutter, debt, shopping, or the size of your home. Maybe it works well for you and maybe it doesn't. What does the Gentle You say? If you are questioning your relationship with alcohol and wondering if it prevents you from showing up and enjoying your life, the only way to know for sure is to try living without it and see how you feel. Then you'll have more information. You can make decisions based on what you experience instead of believing everything you think about alcohol. When I tried experimenting with taking breaks from things like alcohol, coffee, sugar, shopping, social media, and other things I wasn't sure about, it gave me the information I needed on how to proceed, based on how I felt instead of *what I thought I would feel*.

The Tiny Steps

These tiny steps are an invitation to trade any resistance or defensiveness for pure curiosity.

   ÷ *Read about it.* Two books that made a big difference for me are *Quit Like a Woman: The Radical Choice to Not Drink in a Culture Obsessed with Alcohol* by Holly Whitaker and *This Naked Mind* by Annie Grace. The Annie Grace book answered every fear, excuse, or reason I had to keep drinking in a gentle way. I didn't feel judged or pressured at all. Holly's book showed me how big alcohol marketed to me as a woman as well as how our pro-alcohol culture kept me in a cycle of drinking. I credit these books for making my foray out of drinking easy. I know it's not everyone's experience, but I never looked back. I didn't crave a drink. I let go with ease.

❖ *Go without.* Try a Dry July or a Sober October, or be sober-curious during your Gentle January. Go thirty or one hundred days (the benefits vary between the two, so if you can go longer, do). See for yourself.

❖ *Try a mocktail.* In terms of beverage options, it's easier than ever to be alcohol-free. You may be able to find alcohol-free versions of your favorite wines, beers, and spirits. You can also create a mocktail at home or order one when you go out. I usually ask for something "ginger-forward" or, when I want to be fancier than tap water, I get sparkling water with lemon. The fear around what other people will think is fading. Alcohol isn't as much of the social fiber as it used to be. If it still feels deeply woven in at family gatherings, remember your boundaries. Remember who you're doing this for (you).

❖ *Consider your support system.* Remember the Gentle Way? Creating a support system is important with all the changes you are making but especially when you are putting down alcohol or another addictive substance. Find people who can inspire you to stay sober and cheer you on along the way.

One Gentle Step

If the tiny steps feel too big, try one gentle step. Don't drink today. Just today.

Permission Slip:

I do not have to explain why I'm not drinking. I can simply say, "My life is better without alcohol."

EIGHT

Less Advice

As you are rewiring and breaking free of the old messaging of "be better, do more, work harder," you make space for the gentler messages like "go slowly, be softer, take care of you." If this works well for you, it can be tempting to want to get everyone you know on board. After all, if it helps you, it's sure to help them! Here's what I want you to remember: You aren't required to pass this information on to anyone. You're especially not required to pass it on to people who you know will be resistant or who simply aren't interested. Not offering unsolicited advice allows you to continue to marinate in the changes you are making instead of spending any spoons trying to convince someone else to do the same. This also goes for your latest diet, exercise program, or spiritual awakening. I used to be that person who got so excited about something that I'd tell everyone they should do it, too. If you want to get your ideas out there without offering unsolicited advice, there are a few things you can do instead of dumping your wisdom all over someone who doesn't want it. Starting a blog worked for me.

Dealing with unsolicited advice is something we all struggle with at one time or another, whether giving or receiving it. Before I wrote this book, I thought about writing a book on setting boundaries. I sent a survey to bemorewithless.com email subscribers and asked, "What do you tolerate on a regular basis because you think you are supposed to?" One answer that came up several times was "dealing with unsolicited advice" about a variety of topics: what I eat, how I parent, my work, what I'm wearing, how I look, what I do with money, and more! From those thousands of responses, I realized that giving unsolicited advice is something we do to each other without thinking about how hard it is on our relationships.

So, ironically, here is some unsolicited advice on not giving unsolicited advice.

1. **You don't have to be so helpful.**
   Anne Lamott says, "Our help is usually not very helpful. Our help is often toxic. And help is the sunny side of control. Stop helping so much. Don't get your help and goodness all over everybody." Oh, ouch! Help is the sunny side of control?! I'll admit, I often think of my advice as being helpful, which is why seeing it through Anne Lamott's eyes is so powerful. It makes me wonder, do I want to help? Or do I want to control the situation? What about you...helpful or controlling? Or maybe a little bit of both?

2. **Ask first.**
   Ask yourself, "Does this person want my advice?" If you aren't sure, ask *them*. You can preface whatever you're about to say with, "Is it OK if I tell you what I think?" or "Do you want my advice?" If they say no, believe them. Don't force your thoughts on them. They don't want it now and maybe never will. (Note: They know you have it, though. If they change their mind, they'll ask.)

3. **Tell first.**

   When you are talking to your people about something, be clear about what you'd like in response. If you don't want advice, say, "I'd like to share this with you and I am not looking for advice," or "I don't want advice or feedback but instead I just want to say this out loud. I want to vent." And then, just to be really clear (and get their buy-in), ask them, "Is that OK with you?" When you do want advice or input, ask for it.

4. **Consider past exchanges.**

   Ask yourself, *Has my advice been well received in this relationship in the past?* If your advice has been routinely dismissed or debated by someone, stop offering it to them. Instead, ask, "How can I help?" Or just listen. Remember, not everything requires a response.

5. **Don't be mistreated.**

   When someone else's advice crosses the line to commenting on your clothing or your body, or says other things that are completely inappropriate, name it. Say, "That's inappropriate." One of my favorite quotes is from author Elizabeth Lesser. She so eloquently says, "Do no harm, take no shit." You may keep in mind that people don't always know what's appropriate, so you can be gentle when you tell them that you're not interested in hearing what they have to say on this topic. They may react badly at first, or be offended. Stand firm. They'll soon realize that you're not withdrawing your love from them; you just don't want to hear what they have to say. Both things can be true at the same time.

6. **Let it go.**

Once you give advice (with permission), let it go. Unless they ask for more support, it's now up to that person to decide what to do with it. You don't get to control how other people receive your words. If you receive advice that doesn't resonate, let it go. If you feel pressured to act or follow through, then you aren't dealing with advice—you are managing someone else's expectations.

7. **Reframe your advice.**

When giving advice, instead of telling others what they *should* do, remind them that this is just what has been helpful for you. Or suggest how you imagine you would move forward in their situation. Reinforce their self-trust: "You know what's best for you."

On the receiving end, when you are blindsided with unsolicited advice that isn't welcome or helpful, simply say, "Thank you for the thoughtful feedback." Then see #6 above. If the advice is harmful or hurtful, see #5.

8. **Don't take advice too seriously.**

When I'm considering advice, especially unsolicited advice, I do a quick scan and ask the following questions:

Is this person qualified to offer this advice? For instance, if someone is offering me medical advice and they are not a medical professional, I'll say, "Thank you," then do my own research.

Why am I so resistant to or bothered by this advice? Often it's because the advice isn't helpful, but sometimes it's because I really need to hear it but I don't want to hear it.

Even though I don't love it all, is there some wisdom I need here? In other words, don't throw the baby out with the bathwater. (That's a terrible saying but perfectly illustrates what I'm going for here.)

9. **Trust yourself.**

    Before you seek advice from others about how to handle a challenging situation, check in with yourself first. If you feel unclear, slow down, take care of yourself, then check in again. Then, if you choose to seek advice from others, check in once more with yourself. Put your hands on your heart, breathe, and ask, "What's best for me?" Trust the answer. If my advice to put your hands on your heart doesn't resonate, don't. Do something else that encourages a connection with the Gentle You.

    If you are a fixer, this is going to be a journey. When I first began to reel in my advice giving, there were many times when I had the *best* advice on the tip of my tongue. Instead of speaking it, I swallowed it. It was hard! But once I had established the habit of keeping my advice to myself in most cases, I started paying attention to it. Was the advice I wanted to share something I had actually tried? Was I walking the walk before offering this advice to others? Or, in fact, was I just telling them to do something I knew I needed to do myself? Maybe my advice was for me all along.

The Tiny Steps

Trade any defensiveness or judgment you may be experiencing for the tiny steps.

- ÷ *Be clear.* Ask for exactly what you want. "I don't want advice. Are you available for me to cry on your shoulder without trying to fix it?" If someone is crying on your shoulder, before you respond, give them permission to be clear. "Do you want me to offer advice or just be here for you?" Honor their answer.

- ÷ *Be intentional.* Before offering advice to someone because you think you want the best for them, ask yourself what you really want. Ask yourself what they really want for themselves. If you aren't sure, ask them. No assumptions.

- ÷ *Take your own advice.* When your words of wisdom pop up for someone else, ask yourself if you could benefit from taking your own advice. Maybe it was for you all along.

One Gentle Step

If the tiny steps feel like advice that you are not up to receiving today, try one gentle step. Keep it simple. If you must offer advice, the very best advice you can offer (to yourself and others) is, *"Be gentle with yourself."*

Permission Slip:

I don't have to solve other people's problems to be helpful or to be a good friend—I can just listen and be there for them.

NINE

Less Organizing

Wait—the simplicity lady wrote a chapter about organizing less? It may surprise you to know that I'm not very organized. That's why living with less works so well for me. There is less to keep track of, less to lose and find, and less to think about. I rarely lose my keys or wonder where my glasses are. (That said, I do occasionally look for my phone while I'm on the phone.) All this isn't for lack of being organized.

I tried to be organized. For years, I diligently sorted and filed things. I even had a label maker and lots of bins and boxes and cabinets from IKEA. It looked nice! It didn't last. Because I was always acquiring more, I always had to do more organizing. Eventually, I got tired of it. I didn't want more stuff for my stuff, I didn't want to get organized, I wanted to live my life. I understand the idea of being organized, and the benefit of having organizational systems and routines. I also see that most of these systems are just created to help us save everything and store more and get more done so we can bask in the glow of our productivity. I don't care about those things anymore.

One of the reasons we are so easily overwhelmed is because we have so much to deal with. By turning your focus from organizing to living with less, you can create more margin so that when bigger things happen, they don't completely upend your life. You need a buffer for the unexpected. And let's face it: If organizing worked, you'd be organized by now.

The problem isn't your organizing skills or the way you manage your time. The problem is that you are dealing with too much. We love to blame ourselves here, especially when comparing our homes, closets, offices, and calendars to the beautiful images we see on Pinterest or in magazines.

Let's come back to the "too much" problem. When you try to organize your closet, your papers, your kitchen, your photos, your email, and your thoughts (among many more things), you'll notice that you have too much. If you have tried to organize any of these categories and they are still not organized, try a different approach. Instead of organizing all that stuff, let go of most of it. Before you organize one more thing, revisit chapter 1 in this section, on home release. Your time will be better spent letting things go instead of trying to organize them for the fortieth or four hundredth time. Please don't think you are alone in living like this; according to *Yahoo! Finance*,[1] the global home organization products market size was valued at $12 billion in 2022 and is projected to reach $15.9 billion by 2030. That means a lot of people are spending money trying to "get organized" instead of getting rid of all that extra stuff. I do think it's important to point out that different stages of life, family sizes, and interests may impact how much stuff you have. And still... you could probably own less.

Why is it we have so much in the first place? Society tells us that we can have it all, and that if we want to demonstrate our success and find true happiness, we *should* have it all. It's the whole myth about how we are supposed to give our kids more than we had. The thing is, there simply isn't room for all of it. Not in a drawer, not in a home, and not in a life. They told us we could have it all, but they forgot to tell us we might not want it all. Is this just a rich person's problem? Nope. For a long time, I was pretty broke (meaning tens of thousands of dollars in debt) and I had way too much stuff.

The Gentle You is probably tired of taking care of all that stuff. Before she simplified her life, Myquillyn Smith, author of *The Cozy Minimalist*, wrote,[2] "My daily routine involves looking through my stuff, putting stuff away, organizing stuff, feeling guilty because I haven't organized other stuff, fussing at my kids because their stuff isn't put away, wading through misplaced stuff in our garage, piling up stuff I'm tired of so we can sell it, packing away stuff I'm really tired of to give it away, asking my husband where he put his stuff, sorting, washing, and drying our stuff, and then dreaming about more stuff that I want and the bigger house I 'need' because my precious stuff won't fit in our current house—I guess it's too small. I never planned on being a stuff manager, it just kind of happened and now that's my job." We've all been here on some level, spending extra time we don't have, annoyed with how much stuff we've got. The next time you try to get organized, or you are tired of being a stuff manager, think about organizing less. Here are a few examples.

PAPERS AND PHOTOS

Instead of trying to organize piles of papers or photos separately, get them all together and go through them at one time, pile by pile. Approaching this project in a gentle way may take a few days or weeks, or you might want to employ a technique called temptation bundling. According to an article in *Forge*,[3] an online publication on personal development, the term "temptation bundling" was coined by the behavior researcher Katherine Milkman[4] and her colleagues in a 2014 study.

Here's how it works: Basically, you "bundle" a source of instant gratification (like checking Instagram or watching an addictive show) with a beneficial but less fun "should" activity (like running on the treadmill, working on a spreadsheet, or . . . going through your piles of papers or photos). In Milkman's study, the researchers gave participants iPods with four audio novels they wanted to listen to—but they could only access the iPod while working out. By and large, the participants' gym attendance increased when an indulgence was tied to it.

To use temptation bundling to help you organize photos or paper, work on piles while you listen to a podcast or watch your favorite movie. Organizational systems will tell you there is a place for everything, but remember: The proper place is often the recycling bin. With each photo or piece of paper you pick up, ask, "Why save?" If you don't have a compelling reason, let it go. I know this can be hard with physical photos. But do you really need fourteen almost identical photos of your friend's birthday party? Do you really need pictures of people you haven't seen or thought about in twenty-five years? You can apply this to digital files, too. In my experience, folders in a filing cabinet and folders on your digital device work the same way. Things go in and they never come out. Before you file or save a document or photo, ask yourself, "WHY?"

EMAIL

For anyone with more than a hundred emails in your inbox, I beg you to do this. Everyone else will benefit, too. When you open your inbox, instead of going through each email and making decisions one at a time, click "Select all" and uncheck the ones you want to keep. While I'm sure there is an exception to this rule, we all get more junk mail than real actionable messages. And, just like with snail mail, we can tell it's junk without opening it. You may be able to save a big chunk of time each day by not thoughtfully going through each message. Instead, select all, quickly unselect to keep what you want to keep, and delete the rest. If the fear of deleting something important prevents you from making quick decisions, remember that if someone wants your attention, they will email you twice (at least).

You may have heard of the Pareto Principle which states that 80% of outcomes come from 20% of causes. I think this applies to our stuff, too. We only wear 20% of the stuff in our closet, answer 20% of our email (if that), and so on. Imagine getting rid of 80% of your closet. Would you even have to organize the other 20%? From experience, I can tell you that the answer is no.

The Tiny Steps

It's time for some tiny steps to help you organize less and enjoy more.

- ❖ *Rethink your next organizing project.* Flip it upside down and instead of putting 100 percent of it where it belongs, get rid of 80 percent and live with 20 percent. From your closet to digital files and everything in between, it's not your job to make sure *all* of it is completely organized. Instead organize only the things you actually use. Let the rest go.
- ❖ *Notice the things you use every single day.* For a few days, make a list of the physical items you use. Some of the same things will appear on every daily list. Give your attention to those things and see if you can release some others, especially the items you own that never make it on a list.

÷· *Assess your level of stuff management.* Can you relate to Myquillyn Smith's description of managing her stuff? More stuff = more cleaning, more insuring, more organizing, and so on. How much time and energy are you spending on your stuff? Wouldn't you like less stuff so you can spend that time somewhere more rewarding?

÷· *Make a big project small.* If you've been upset with yourself because you haven't organized your paper, photos, craft supplies, or another category of stuff, make it small. Perhaps for now, because you aren't doing anything with it, you simply put it all together in a box or a bin and deal with it later. And if you don't deal with it in a year or so, perhaps you can decide just to let the whole thing go.

One Gentle Step

If you aren't up for the tiny steps today, choose one gentle step instead. Identify something you enjoy watching or listening to that you can use for future temptation bundling.

Permission Slip:

I will stop glamorizing the idea of getting organized and live with less instead.

TEN

Release Your Pain

Where do you hold your pain? Maybe in your shoulders, your hips, or somewhere else in your body? I kept my pain in my journals. The only way I can write books, articles, or anything else for public consumption is by first writing down my pain. I write down my joy, too, or anything else that is swirling around in my brain. It's that swirling that gets in the way of my writing. I get too focused on the thoughts. *What's for dinner? I can't believe he said that! I'm not writing enough. I suck at writing. Why am I writing? I forgot to take the clothes out of the dryer. Is she mad at me? I need to make a list, make a meal plan, check in with my team, call my daughter, take a walk, go to bed earlier. My neck hurts. I should think about spending less time on my phone.*

On and on the swirling and spiraling goes. This is why I journal. I don't journal for memory keeping, at least not until recently (I'll tell you more about that later). I journal to move all of the motion and emotion from my body and brain to paper. I journal with pen and paper rather than on a computer or other digital device. If there isn't pen and paper to be found and I have to move some thoughts around, I'll make a quick audio note on my phone—which reminds me, I have a handful of those I need to delete. I never, ever listen to them. I could stop writing and listen to them, but then I couldn't be in the moment of clarity that I'm in right now. I could reread my journals but, again, they'll remove me from right now.

And I've started to see that there's no real value in hanging on to these old thoughts and ideas. The only reason would be to revisit other moments, other thoughts, other drama I experienced or created. I tried this once when I was having a hard time with someone. I used my journals as proof that I was right to dig into my hurt and anger, that my pain was justified. I told myself I was looking for patterns, but I wasn't. I was looking for pain. It was like the teenage me listening to the saddest songs after a breakup. I wanted to roll around in the sadness. It worked, too. The pain I revisited made me sad and angry. It made me mistrustful. It felt like having a bad dream about someone and then waking up angry at them for something that wasn't even really happening anymore.

I write a little bit every day in my journals. When I'm in more joy or more pain (or if something really hard or something very cool happened), I write more. Then, every once in a while, I release my pain and past feelings and thoughts by shredding or burning my journals. I release them with a great amount of peace and love. I honor that these things happened, and I recognize that holding on to them, even if I'm not rereading or re-experiencing them, is a disservice to me and to today's thoughts, feelings, joy, and even pain. Instead, I release all of it to make room for more of it. I want to look out the window and notice the beauty. I want to talk to a friend on the phone and be fully present. I want to engage in my relationships, recognizing that holding on to every single past detail holds me back from evolving into something more connected. I want to check in on my heart with my right now–ness instead of the version of me that holds on to everything from before.

For me, when I kept the journals, it added a lens or a filter to how I looked at my relationships and life. I want to be a filter-free gal. Sometimes the Gentle Me was afraid to let go of my pain. Would I remember it? I took a deep breath and let go anyway. Now, the memories come and go without a tight grip on my heart. The pain softens around the edges and fades. I realize I don't have to hold on to heal. Of course, there are and will be more traumatic events that may require deeper introspection, therapy, and other treatment that burning a journal won't erase. Seek the help you need and deserve.

If you've been saving your journals without a plan, I'd invite you to ask yourself why. Are you saving them to write a book? Are you holding on because you want friends and family to read them when you are gone? And if you are, have you considered the impact? Will your journals cause harm to others? Do you need them to understand who you are? Are you afraid you won't create new memories, thoughts, feelings, joy, and pain?

I've worked with people who want to release their journals because their answers to these questions suggested that was the best course of action, but they were concerned that they would forget what happened. That might be the case. You may not remember certain things, or not in the detail that you described in your journal. I'm OK with that. Being OK with it has become much easier since I've decided I don't need to prove to myself who I am anymore. I don't need receipts.

If you are interested but not completely sold on the idea, I recommend creating a journal about all of your journals. It's a little meta, but review your journals, pull out any crucial bits of information, then transfer those to the new journal. Hopefully you can consolidate several journals into one. My preference is to release them, but I do understand that, especially if you are considering this idea for the first time, you might need an in-between option. It's sort of like when we talked about hiding your stuff before donating it when decluttering. Another example is when I was struggling with letting go of sentimental items before decluttering them. I took photos of them first (and then never looked at the photos). Sometimes that in-between step helps.

If what's holding you back is the fear of not remembering, consider how you want to spend your time now and how you may want to spend it in the future. Will you want to spend it frustrated that you can't remember things, and trying to unearth your past? Or will you want to read a book, spend time with people you love, play a game, watch your favorite movie, or learn a new skill? I want to sip a coffee or a hot chocolate and watch the snow fall in the winter. Or watch the water sparkle with sunlight on a summer hike. This is another practice in letting go so you can be free to show up for your life in whatever state it is and whatever state you are in right now. If you want people to remember what you accomplished in your life, leave them your résumé. If you want to leave them with a glimpse of your day-to-day life, try a five-year journal, writing a few sentences a day. That's what I'm using on a daily basis now as a way to capture a little bit of what happens each day. If you want people to remember your heart, treat them gently and treat yourself gently.

If you don't journal, where do you hold your thoughts, feelings, joy, and pain? Where do you store your past? If you feel it in your body and don't know what to do with it, revisit the advice from somatic therapist Rachel Shanken on page 58. Being gentle isn't ignoring that the pain happened. It's not dismissing your life experience; it's only asking the Gentle You if holding on continues to serve you. If it's too heavy, find a way to release it. If you want to be light, you have to let go.

Years ago, when I wrote about burning my journals and letting go of sentimental items, I received the following message (reprinted with permission):

Hi Courtney,

In one of your recent posts you wrote: "One of the reasons I shred or burn my journals is to symbolically let go of my stories; of stress, pain and drama. This allows me to focus on what's happening right now instead of what I thought was happening in the past."

I love the idea of shredding my journals, but I have this tight hold on all of them (as I do on all of my memorabilia items that I choose to keep). I feel like if they disappear, then I will disappear. Like they are proof of my life and thoughts and goals, etc. That is where all of the meaning is. I can't seem to let go of them, because then it will mean I don't exist and I lose everything.

Any suggestions or words to share to focus on the present and look to the future, and not be afraid to let go of these reflections of the past? It's really, really, really hard to let go! How do I separate the meaning of my life from these "things" that are just reflections I've collected along the way?

Thank you!
Christina

I knew how Christina was feeling. I used to feel the same way. I started saving my memories as proof of life in elementary school. I kept saving them through school and adulthood. I moved them from state to state, apartment to apartment. Even when I started to declutter and live more simply, I didn't consider letting go of my sentimental items. And then, when there was nothing left to let go of, I took another look at the sentimental stuff. I wasn't displaying it or enjoying it. I was just saving it. Saving it as proof that I had lived. I wrote back.

> Hi Christina,
>
> I can appreciate how you feel and am glad you shared this with me. It took me a while to figure this out for myself but once I did, letting go got so much easier.
>
> The meaning of my life is not in what I save or keep, it's in how I live. The meaning IS the living. So now I live instead of proving that I've lived by the stuff I saved.
>
> xo,
> Courtney

IN OTHER WORDS...

Instead of proving that you have lived, live.

Instead of proving that you have loved, love.

I'm not pretending to be a great philosopher here to share the meaning of life. I don't know what it is. But I am confident that I know what it isn't. The meaning of life isn't all the stuff I collected over my life. And it's not the stuff I leave behind. Not even the really good stuff.

The Tiny Steps

These tiny steps will help you consider the idea of releasing your pain with more ease and grace.

- *Collect your journals.* Pull together all of your journals and brain dumps. Get them all in one place so you can see what you are dealing with. Without opening them, see how you feel about them today. How long have you had them and what is your plan for them?
- *Ask the questions.* Why are you saving them? Have you ever reread them? What do you hope to gain by reading them? How would you feel if they were gone? Also revisit the questions I mentioned earlier:
  - Are you saving them to write a book?
  - Are you holding on because you want friends and family to read them when you are gone? If you are, have you considered the impact? Will your journals cause harm to others?
  - Do you need your journals to understand who you are?
  - Are you afraid you won't create new memories, thoughts, feelings, joy, and pain? How do you want to spend your time?
- *Set a burn date.* Choose a time and place to burn your journals if you can burn them safely. Otherwise consider shredding them. Honor yourself and your past in any way you'd like as you release your pain.

One Gentle Step

If burning or shredding your journals feels like the last thing you want to do, simply notice your resistance.

Maybe it's not time, or perhaps something else has a hold on you. Don't push yourself, just be with yourself.

Permission Slip:

I release my pain and past thoughts and feelings to make room for new life experiences.

ELEVEN

Less Regret

The saddest conversations I have are with people who live in a pool of regret. Some even regret that they regret so much. It is always a good reminder to me to try and make choices that don't lead to regret and, when that doesn't work out (since I still haven't figured out how to be the perfect human), to give myself the grace to let it go. It's also encouraged me to consider what I'm doing now that I might regret when I'm older. These are things you can stop doing when you are 23, 35, 62, 84, or any age. More important, when you do, you'll start enjoying your life more right now.

Living with regret can be very painful. Dan Pink, author of many books, including *The Power Of Regret: How Looking Backward Moves Us Forward*, suggests that instead of minimizing regret, we learn how to optimize it. He says, "There's a reason we experience negative emotions. They're useful if we treat them right. Regret, you don't want to wallow in it. You don't want to ruminate over it. But if you think of it as a signal, as information, as a knock at the door, it is a powerfully transformative emotion."[1]

Regret has a way of building up. When we live in the sadness and disappointment of regret instead of recognizing it for what it is and learning from it, we're likely to make other decisions that we'll eventually regret. But sometimes our regret can come from subtle habits we barely notice we have. Here are some common ways we allow regret to pile up in our lives that you can let go of— knowledge is power.

1. APOLOGIZING FOR TAKING CARE OF YOURSELF

When we apologize for taking care of ourselves, we often end up compromising the care we know we need. From staying out late or overscheduling ourselves, to tolerating behavior that doesn't contribute to our overall health, we save taking care of us for later, for tomorrow. And then later, we feel run-down or even get sick because we didn't do what we knew we needed to do. That moment, when you think you don't have time or approval to take care of yourself, is the exact moment you need to take care of yourself.

Not apologizing for taking care of yourself may mean not sharing and not overexplaining your actions. Don't regret not taking care of yourself in fear of what others may think.

2. SPENDING SO MUCH TIME ON YOUR PHONE

The time we spend on our phones is getting in the way of creativity, connection, focus, sleep, and more. If we don't stop now, there will be a day when we regret not paying attention to our relationships, the projects we didn't pursue, the world we never saw, and our general inability to pay attention to anything for very long, all because we were hooked into our phones, for the sake of a quick dopamine hit (or just our bad habits).

3. TRYING TO BE RIGHT

These days many of the things I used to need to be right about are not even a little bit important to me. I just don't have the time and energy to be right, to argue my point, or to engage in conversations about everything, especially when others are committed to misunderstanding me. Being right just doesn't feel as worthwhile as being connected, rested, and well. I'd rather notice how lovely my first cup of coffee of the day smells, pick up some flowers on my way home, or laugh with my daughter. I know that if I invest so much of myself trying to be right, I will regret it. Can you relate? Have you ever felt so committed to being right or getting the last word that you ruined a conversation or a relationship? As Dan Pink suggests, if you do feel regret, use it as a signal and make a change.

4. STOP SAYING YES WHEN
YOU WANT TO SAY NO

I don't know who needs to hear this but . . . you are allowed to say no even when you aren't busy. You can stay home instead of going to an event that sounds dreadful or even really fun but you're just too tired. You can say no when your heart says no. You can say no when you need to take care of yourself (see #1). You can say no when you crave more peace, quiet, or anything else you want for your life. If you don't, you'll likely regret all those moments when you really wanted to say yes but didn't have the energy or time. If you don't have time for what matters, stop doing things that don't.

5. STOP ASSUMING THAT EVERYONE
AND EVERYTHING IS AGAINST YOU

And if you must make assumptions, assume positively. Assume that everyone is cheering you on and that everything is working in your favor. When we assume that other people are having thoughts about our lives, our actions, our interests, and our behaviors, we change. We change who we are for something that may not even be happening. The only way to live in alignment with your own heart, and to avoid the regret of pretending to be something you are not only to please others, is to keep coming back to yourself. The Gentle You knows better.

6. WANTING THINGS FOR OTHER PEOPLE MORE
THAN THEY WANT THEM FOR THEMSELVES

Pushing your agenda and expectations on the people you love in the name of "knowing what's best for them" will end in regret. Even if they bend to your will, you'll know your relationship is being built on conditions instead of love, support, and encouragement. This rarely begins with malicious intent, but the impact it has can be devastating. You can break this habit and avoid future regret by noticing when it's happening. When you notice it, write it down and see if there is something useful for you.

7. SAYING MEAN THINGS TO YOURSELF

We say things to ourselves that we would never say to someone else or tolerate hearing from anyone else. Our inner critics can be real jerks. I don't know about you, but telling myself how much I suck at something has never made me better at whatever that something is. When your inner critic isn't being helpful, acknowledge the thought. Say to that voice, "I hear you and I don't receive that." Then, just as a reminder of who's in charge of you, follow that up with saying something sweet and gentle to yourself. Keep doing this, and eventually the mean version of your inner critic won't show up so much.

8. GIVING UP ON OUR DREAMS

This may be something you are regretting already. Perhaps you didn't think you had the talent, time, or other resources to pursue your dreams. If there is something you are curious about or excited about now, define the dream. Write it down and ask concrete questions like, "What will it take to make this dream a reality?" If the list feels too long or too out of reach, make it smaller. What's a step you can take today that will bring you closer? Who's living your dream who you might be able to learn from? You still have time for dreams. Maybe a dream you used to have isn't possible, but that doesn't mean you should stop dreaming. What version of that dream could still be available to you? Don't give up on your dreams and don't stop dreaming up new dreams.

You may see yourself as already experiencing some of the regrets on this list. I know I do. If you do, too, celebrate your openness and willingness to look at what may not be serving you, now or in the future. Perhaps with some extra awareness and small shifts you can be gentler with yourself and regret less.

The Tiny Steps

These tiny steps will help you gently examine your relationship with regret.

⁙ *Recognize the difference between guilt and regret.* We often use these words interchangeably, but they are different things. Generally, guilt is feeling bad about having done something wrong (and, often what we think of as "guilt" isn't guilt at all, it's discomfort—more on this back in chapter 9, "Redefine Your Guilt," in the "Rest" section). Regret is simply wishing that you had done things differently.

⁙ *Look for lessons.* If you can identify something you regret, look for the lessons. Will you make a change, or think differently about something based on this regret? Can you keep the lesson and release the regret?

⁙ *Stop punishing yourself.* Would you continually punish a friend if they made the same mistake? No? Then stop punishing yourself.

⁙ *Avoid regret.* Choose one of the above recommendations. Or if you see something that could go in the direction of something you may regret in the future, course-correct now.

One Gentle Step

If this chapter sent you into a regret spiral, skip the tiny steps for now. Start here with one gentle step. Make a quick list of regrets. The simple action of writing them down will provide some relief. Later, when you are ready for more healing, you can come back to the tiny steps.

Permission Slip:

I can acknowledge regret and let it go because I don't deserve to suffer anymore.

A LITTLE MORE ON LESS

Before we continue with the next section and the next set of gentle practices to help you connect with and nourish the Gentle You, I want to talk a little more about Less. Simplicity has been a guiding practice for me since my MS diagnosis in 2006. It was also the tipping point of so much more. During an exam, my neurologist told me that I was standing on the edge of a cliff. He said, "You need to decide if you are going to keep going as you are, or back away from the edge by making some changes in your life." While he didn't suggest specific lifestyle changes, I knew that eliminating stress would be part of the steps I took. What I didn't know back then was that simplifying and living with less would make the biggest difference in reducing stress. Fewer items in my home, on my calendar, and running around in my mind gave me space to breathe and heal. That was all I wanted. I wanted to be well. I wanted to feel good. I wanted to be able to show up for my family. Living with less gave me all of that and so much more.

As I considered the edge of the cliff I was standing on, I needed to make some big decisions and changes in my life in order to take care of myself. Whether your edge of a cliff is the end of a relationship, a health crisis, financial stress, or all of the above, instead of distancing yourself with more, try less. I once heard someone say that trauma is not what happens to you but all the things you do trying to fill the space to put distance between you and what happened. What if we stopped trying so hard to fill those spaces? I gave myself all of the space, healing, presence, and joy I wanted with the Gentle Way. Remember? Why + Tiny Steps + Support. Instead of filling the spaces, ask the Gentle You what she needs. Then give yourself permission to ease your pain and solve your problems not with doing more and owning more but by doing less and owning less. Be more with less.

PART III

RISE

Becoming the Gentle You doesn't mean you have to withdraw from the world. You don't have to stop striving for what you want or stop caring. Quite the opposite. Your connection with the Gentle You will now serve as the foundation for realizing your dreams and living the life you crave. The Gentle You becomes the solid ground beneath your feet, especially when it otherwise feels shaky. The gentle practices from the last two sections have led you here. They've been supporting your journey to the Gentle You and they continue to unfold through this third and final section, where you will focus on a gentler way to rise up in the world and accomplish all that you want to accomplish, not by pushing through but by easing through. In this final section of the book, you will take all the knowledge you have gathered from the practices in this book so that you can go forward and create the slower, more peaceful life you are hungry for.

Now that you have defined your rhythm of rest, less, and rise, everything comes together. It's not that you have one season of rest, or one big less session and *then* rise, rise, rise. Instead, it's a rhythm or a cycle. It happens again and again and, yes, again. When you are struggling, it's likely that your ratio of Rest:Less:Rise isn't serving you. These stages of the Gentle You are all deeply connected. In your life, each stage is only as strong as the weakest one. You can't make up for skimping on rest by getting rid of an extra pair of shoes. You can't push harder to rise by piling more onto an overly full plate. We've all attempted these shortcuts and become frustrated when they've led us back to where we started, feeling even more defeated. We go through these gentle stages when we are navigating a transition in our lives, when we get sick, when we are processing hard world events or a personal crisis. We even move through the gentle stages with work and other endeavors.

Creative projects like writing this book have been no exception. Without the rest-less-rise path, we often fight and resist before finally realizing that everything takes its time. We can't hurry or push our way through. Creating something new responds well to nurturing the Gentle You through the cycles of rest, less, and rise. At first there is a lull, a quieting and time to notice, retreat, and restore (rest). Next, we make space by removing the things that are taking up time we'd rather devote to another aspect of our lives (less), then we create (rise). I've been through several cycles just writing this book. Rest, less, rise; then after a writing session, I rest again. Then I clear my calendar and obligations (less) and write again (rise).

I should mention that this process is rarely as flowy or linear as we want it to be. Sometimes, we have to rise unexpectedly. We have our usual daily risings (like waking up to start the day, taking care of our families and regular obligations), but then there are the surprise moments where we are called to rise, from a last-minute request from someone you love to an emergency or crisis. When I was working on the last parts of this book, I took a month off. My plan—the one where I think I control everything—was to take a break from writing and come back with fresh eyes. I spent most of my time off traveling, hiking, and spending time with family. Two weeks before my return and plan to rise with fresh eyes, I got sick and broke my foot (both on the same day). Even though I knew I'd ultimately let the Gentle Me lead the way, for the first forty-eight hours I shut her out. I was sick, sad, bothered, and, frankly, kind of pissed off. What about my plan? My injured foot and spirit reminded me of one of my clients, Janet.

Often, when it's time to rise, we rush in. When I spoke to her on a video call, Janet was frustrated. She had started the fall very excited to declutter her whole house. She felt inspired and motivated—now was the time! She began with her closet. She followed the steps for starting the Project 333 wardrobe challenge and moved all her clothes to the bed in her guest room. I usually recommend using your own bed, but her plan was to move everything out, pack for a vacation, and get back to it when she returned from her trip. She had been looking forward to visiting national parks in Utah to hike with her son and husband, but in the back of her mind she was holding excitement for her big decluttering project. In our call, weeks later, she told me, "I couldn't wait to get home and hit the ground running." Ahh, one of my favorite ways of saying "push yourself until you burn out."

Well, sadly, on day one of her vacation, Janet *did* hit the ground running. She fell while hiking and suffered a terrifying brain bleed, a banged-up face, and other injuries. She was going to be OK, but to help her recover, her doctor gave her this prescription: "Do nothing." Janet felt the irony; all of the messages she had heard from me in our few short weeks of working together rushed in. Slow down. Tiny Steps. Put yourself in time-out. When she got home, she was still on doctor's orders to do nothing. As she started to feel better, she wanted to do something, do more, get back to it. She began to resist the slower approach. That was when we had our video call.

This story may sound familiar to you. Maybe it wasn't a fall, but getting a cold, getting worn down at work, lost in breaking news like my friend Marsha in chapter 8 in the "Rest" section, or something else that left you depleted. Still, you want to take action and do something, anything! You want to be ready to rise...but you just aren't. Usually, you learn this the hard way. Moving forward, notice if you are doing things the hard way. Are you pushing through? Are you refusing to accept what's really going on? If so, extend grace to yourself and invite the Gentle You in to support yourself, to love yourself, to help yourself navigate your way back to where you want to be. Doing that is the route to trusting that you know what's best for you. It may not be what you want. It may not be what you had planned, but it's where you are. It's who you are. It's how you move forward with ease.

It's natural to want to rise too soon and too fast. As I mentioned, those societal messages run deep. For instance, even if you didn't intentionally rest but were stuck home after getting sick, and all your body would allow was rest, as soon as you can get back to it you try to rise from a place of panic. We often act as if we have to make up for every moment we weren't doing things. We have to catch up! This could be happening on a smaller scale every morning when you rise out of bed. Do you rush into your day? Or do you move into it from a place of being gentle with yourself and others? Starting with a rush almost always ends in some kind of crash. If you think you should be doing more rising because it looks like everyone out there is on the rise-rise-rise path, remember the liryae quote: "There is literally nothing in nature that blooms all year long, so do not expect yourself to do so."

This is the last section of the book, but it doesn't mean we've only been doing the work of the Gentle You just so that we can rise. Some books about rest and doing less are really a sly productivity hack to get you to continue to chase more. *Gentle* is not that. While, in my experience, letting go of control tends to allow more into my life, the real benefit of this process is becoming the Gentle Me. There are no subliminal productivity messages here. Rising is simply part of the cycle.

At this stage of the Gentle journey, it's time to not only rise but to rise differently. Instead of getting swept up by the excitement of something new, or comparing your next step to another, or reverting to old habits like pushing through, it's time to rise gently. As you move through these gentle practices and start to rise in your own life, remember, it doesn't have to be all sweat and tears and hard work. There may be some of that, but these aren't the core ingredients of a gentle rising. You can get where you need to go softly, gently, sweetly. Stay connected to how you feel. Give yourself what you need. Do you need more rest? More less? Or more frequent reminders to slow down and be intentional? Do you need connection and community or quiet time to put your hands on your heart?

When I was ready to rise and write this last section of *Gentle*, I didn't have the words right away, so I went looking for them. There I am poring through books and scouring the internet looking for inspiration when I remember these words from Rumi: "When I run after what I think I want, my days are a furnace of stress and anxiety; if I sit in my own place of patience, what I need flows to me, and without pain. From this I understand that what I want also wants me, is looking for me and attracting me. There is a great secret here for anyone who can grasp it." I put down my research and my deadlines and my stress and go for a hike. My hike ends at one of the most magnificent patios in Utah overlooking Albion Basin, and the Alta Mountain view pulls me in. I feel euphoric. I sit down with a warm cup of coffee on this cool mountain morning, and I let Rumi's words course through me. *If I sit in my own place of patience* . . . Previously, I would have chased after what I needed. I would have pushed and efforted my way through but today, I sit, I wait, I finally grasp this great secret. Even though I won't write for a few days, the words are writing themselves inside of me while everything around me falls away. I am softly rising.

ONE

Prioritize the Gentle You

Prioritizing the Gentle You means finally making yourself the priority of your own life. You've done more than enough for the people around you. You have sacrificed what you know you need and want in service of everyone and anyone that is not you. You've probably put yourself at the bottom of every list (if you even put yourself on the list). It's enough. Unless you decide to be your priority and to do what is best for you, then at some point your well will run dry (and maybe it already has). Who else is going to do this for you? What are you waiting for? Aren't you deserving of the exceptional treatment you give everyone else? The answer is yes. Not because you earned it. Because you are worth it. You are worthy of taking care of, being kind to, and showering yourself with love and adoration. You are worthy of being gentle. Even when you don't feel worthy of those things, you still are. Why resist?

Check in. In terms of priority in your life, where do you see the Gentle You? Notice if you are too focused on balance, trying to fit it all in and get it all done. Answer the following questions to see what's really going on:

- When you make a list of things that are important to you in life, where do you appear on the list?

169

- Are you even on the list?
- What was the last kind thing you said to yourself?
- What were the last gentle words you said to yourself or someone else? Do you even remember?

We know how to be gentle but extending gentleness to ourselves doesn't come easy. You've been kind to others and encouraged them not to be too hard on themselves. You've likely had a sweet word or action for a child—or how about the way you talk to your pet or a sweet dog you encounter in the park? "Who's a good boy?" "You are such a sweet floof." When my grand-dogs, Stanley or Caspian, finish their dinner, sneeze, or roll over and let me pet their bellies, I always say, in my sweetest, gentlest voice, "Oh my goodness! Look at you!" I treat that sneeze as if they had just learned how to speak French. They get all of my adoration. Later that same day, if I forget to do something, the words that rush in on autopilot are, "You are such an idiot! What's wrong with you?" I can't think of one other person or being on the planet I would use those words with.

When was the last time you finished a meal, looked at your belly, and said to yourself, "You are so freaking adorable and amazing"? Stop waiting for someone else to tell you what you need to hear. Tell yourself. It was a long time before I could tell myself what I needed to hear. I thought it made me self-absorbed, conceited, or full of myself. I thought it was definitely *not* the behavior of a good girl. When I first tried saying kind things to myself—the things I needed to hear—it felt weird. I didn't believe it. Now, I trust myself. At a recent doctor's visit, my neurologist asked me if I had experienced any personality changes (I promise it's a routine question). I answered, "My personality just keeps getting better and better."

My neurologist and I both laughed as I said it. And even though no one else has ever told me this, I just know it's true. I'm more me. I'm the Gentle Me.

While there will always be people and projects who want and/or need your attention and gentle feedback, you need it more. You need it first. You need it now. Make time and space for the Gentle You by putting yourself at the top of the list. You could wake up a little earlier to take care of you. You might find other ways to prioritize yourself.

Here are some other suggestions:

- Cancel your next appointment.
- Go to bed early.
- Schedule a pedicure.
- Turn off your phone.
- Take a bath or shower.
- Call your best friend (the one who knows how to love you).
- Read a book.
- Go for a walk.
- Write something down that really pissed you off, then tear it up.
- Bake something for your neighbor (and for yourself).
- Do nothing.
- Get support.
- Before a hard conversation, make sure to hydrate and eat.
- Laugh.
- Cry.
- Sit still.
- Don't apologize for putting yourself first.

- Write a love letter to yourself today. Write one to your past self or future self.
- Put your hands on your heart and ask, "What do I want?"
- Give yourself permission to want what you want.
- Reject these ideas in favor of something that sounds better to you.

Self-care doesn't always mean adding something. Taking away a habit or something else that isn't serving you is also powerful. Give yourself permission to stop. You don't *have* to stop. You *get* to stop.

- Stop pushing.
- Stop complaining.
- Stop drinking alcohol.
- Stop controlling.
- Stop overextending yourself.
- Stop compromising your heart.
- Stop saying yes when you want to say no.
- Stop caring so much about what other people think about you.
- Stop proving yourself.
- Stop doubting yourself.

Decide what you need to stop to enjoy your life even more. Then give yourself permission to stop. It's a privilege to remove things that are holding us back. I'm so grateful that we get to stop; when we stop doing things like this, and we start tapping into what makes us feel good, what nourishes us, what makes us smile and allows us to relax, that's when we make space for the gentlest side of ourselves.

TOO BUSY FOR THIS?

If you are laughing (or also maybe crying) and thinking, *I don't have time to take care of myself. I'm too busy*, it's time to reassess. What is so important right now, that you have to sacrifice your own happiness, not to mention your physical and mental health? I've talked to enough sick people who wore themselves into exhaustion because they were too busy to prioritize themselves. I was a sick person who wore myself into exhaustion because I was too busy to prioritize myself. This story only ends well when you start putting yourself first. I don't deny that there are fuller times and situations in life, like those with children, aging parents, illness, job loss, financial stress, a breakup, or a breakdown. Is it possible that, even in those times and situations, we could at least be gentle (or gentl*er*) with ourselves? There is nothing to lose by being gentle during a challenging time.

Instead, our natural reaction is to insert ourselves into every moment of every situation as if nothing would get done without us, while completely neglecting what is best for us. We so desperately want to be in control that we attempt to orchestrate an outcome that simply is not up to us. We push and shove against reality only to suffer more. What is the gentler choice? Where is the Gentler You? If you have to go through this shit anyway, can you do it with more peace and ease and less struggle and stress? If you can do that, will you be more resilient and energetic, and have more to give yourself and everyone around you? Even if the only benefit was feeling a little bit better as you were going through what you were going through, wouldn't that be enough of a reason for this shift?

This is as good a time as any to do what is best for you. Maybe it's the very best time. Tomorrow morning when you wake up, instead of mentally scrolling your to-do list or actually scrolling the internet, say to yourself, *Now, I'll do what's best for me.* If you aren't sure what that is, get curious. Ask yourself:

- What's best for me right now?
- What's the best way for me to start my day?
- If I have to do something for someone else, how can I shift something so that it's good for me, too (or at least better than it was before)?
- What is the next gentle step?

When you notice that you are overthinking these questions, slow down, get still, and rest. Don't force your answers. See what comes to you. It's OK not to know right away. It's OK to change your mind. It's OK to trust the answers that come up. Be your first priority by taking care, listening, and moving forward in a way that means something to *you*.

The Tiny Steps

These tiny steps will help you begin to prioritize yourself consistently. You decide how to make them part of your life, but I recommend one at a time, practicing day by day until it feels like the right time to start the next one.

- *Ask for help.* Once you're able to create time and space to listen to the inner knowledge you already have, you'll find there's a lot you can give yourself; in the meantime, perhaps what you need most right now is help and support from someone else. Ask yourself, is the next gentle step asking for help? If you're able to hire someone to help with things you can't get to around the house, or even simple daily activities, do that. If getting dinner on the table feels impossible, try a meal kit service or ask a friend or neighbor to swap, or get something delivered. During a challenging year at his university, my nephew Axel and his circle of friends each cooked dinner one night for their group. They had a home-cooked meal every night of the week, but each person only had to cook once. You could ask a friend to sit with you while you work through something challenging. When you ask for help so that you can take time to heal, you allow your future self to experience life in gentler, more joyful ways.

⁜ *Consider therapy.* I don't know anyone who wouldn't benefit from time with a good therapist. If you aren't sure, absolutely read *Maybe You Should Talk to Someone* by Lori Gottlieb. My friend Tammy felt lonely during the pandemic. Like many of us, she felt disconnected from the world, even as an introvert who enjoys her alone time. Phone calls with friends were nice, but they didn't replace being able to connect in person. Because she had a good practice of prioritizing her well-being, she recognized that she needed help. Her feelings of loneliness were beginning to affect her sleep and mental health. She couldn't find a therapist who would see her in person, so she tried an online therapy app. She met with a virtual therapist weekly who helped her. Even though it was more than a year before she could meet up with friends again, the therapist helped her work through how she was feeling. Just vocalizing her struggles helped her to feel better.

If you can't afford a therapist yourself, ask your doctor if getting therapy or counseling is something you can access through your health care plan, or ask therapists if they offer a sliding scale to meet your needs.

❖ *Take time off.* When you have a fever, you take the day off. If you broke your arm, you'd probably need at least a day off. But what about when your heart hurts or your mind is overwhelmed? Why do we so easily dismiss invisible symptoms as something we have to silently suffer through or try to ignore? Those things call for time off, too. If you don't work for someone who would understand that, tell them you don't feel well—and consider if you might be able to work for someone who would understand.

One Gentle Step

If those tiny steps felt overwhelming or you aren't sure if this is the right time to rise, consider one gentle step. Keep a notepad and pen next to your bed. Either before you fall asleep or before you get out of bed in the morning, write yourself a permission slip to do one tiny thing today that's just for you.

Permission Slip:

I CAN GIVE MYSELF PERMISSION. I'm putting this in all CAPS because this is a big one—the biggest. Always give yourself permission to do what you need to do to take care of yourself. In the name of prioritizing you, it's time to give yourself permission. Sometimes we withhold the most basic things from ourselves because we forget that we can just have it, do it, or take it. Give yourself permission to do anything that helps you to rise in a way that doesn't wear you out. If you know you need and deserve more permission around something and you can't figure out how to extend that grace to yourself, email support@bemorewithless.com. Write "PERMISSION" in the subject line and tell me what you know is best for you. I will give you permission to give yourself permission.

TWO

Be Gentle Anytime

Very recently, I had two hard life experiences, both at the same time: I injured my wrist and, shortly after, my seventeen-year-old cat, Wilbur, got sick. Like, really sick. I took him to the vet and learned that he wasn't going to get better. Four days later, I held him at the vets' office, crying, kissing his face, and saying goodbye. That week, I was in a bad place. My wrist was in pain, I was feeling frustrated with my lack of mobility, and I was grieving. I was not in a gentle space. There were ungentle things going on in the news, too, and I felt overwhelmed and unable to shut them out while I got on with my work. And yet, I had a deadline to write a book proposal—something I don't enjoy doing even when everything's going great. For a moment I thought, *I can't do this. I have to wait until everything is better. I have to fix everything. I need more perfect circumstances before I can work on this book about being gentle, since right now, I myself am unable to be gentle.*

Has that ever happened to you? You are about to start something new or do something that requires your calm energy, but you wait, hoping for a better time, the "right" time. Thankfully, it didn't take me long to laugh at myself, and the idea of waiting until everything was calm and perfect. Because... are things *ever* calm and perfect? How many years would I need to finish this book if I was only writing during the best of times? Could I ever even finish it?!

I started to get curious: What if I could carve out some gentle time and a gentle place in the midst of this chaos? Even while I was in pain, even while I was grieving. So, I made a Gentle playlist full of my favorite soothing music and gave myself permission to just do a little bit. I also decided if I felt like I was forcing anything, I would take a break. Creating that space helped me write the book proposal with compassion and love. It also added a layer of ease to everything else. I was still hurting, I was still grieving, but I also made room to feel hopeful at the same time.

It always surprises me how things like hope and hurting are not mutually exclusive. I took a gentle approach to the book writing, too. As the proposal came together, or if I made a beautiful dinner, or if I felt really good for a particular moment even when I was really sad, I thought, *How fascinating that I can be gentle and experience creative flow, joy, and love at the very same time that my feelings are scattered in another direction.* I was able to be gentle and feel unpressured while writing. I hope that, as a result, you feel some gentleness in these words.

Big projects, habit changes, and other things we want to do often happen while lots of other things seem to be going in the wrong direction. Something is always beginning while something else is ending. As one thing falls apart, another comes together. I know I'm being vague here. It's because that's how life is: something and everything all at once. Being gentle is not an all-or-nothing situation. You can't wait for the perfect, calm moment to become the Gentle You. Just because you can't be gentle every time or everywhere doesn't mean you can't be gentle sometimes, somewhere. Since being gentle with ourselves doesn't come naturally, it's often in our moments of pain that we forget to soften, and take care. Whether we're grieving the loss of someone we love, faced with our own health crisis, or dealing with job loss, a tragedy, or another significant blow, instead of taking care, we dive deeper into despair. But even while you are struggling, hurting, or suffering, it is possible to create a moment that's easier, lighter, and more gentle.

Don't force gentleness, allow it. Make room for it. Be open to it. When I say, "Don't force it," I think about people who smile when they are sad just because someone told them it would make them feel better. Anytime I try that, it makes me even more upset. Now, my face is lying, which makes me feel worse than I did to begin with. When I do smile in pain, it's not to please others. It's self-preservation. Brené Brown suggests that if your healing depends on someone else's response, you're not ready to share your pain with others yet. In an interview on Elizabeth Gilbert's podcast *Magic Lessons*,[1] Brown says, "The only stories I share with the public in my writing or speaking are stories that I have really processed. My healing is not contingent on your opinion of those stories." When I'm not ready for the questions, suggestions, and genuine offers of help that come with my admission of being in pain, I'll smile or stay home.

You also need space to be gentle. When our lives are crammed with too much stuff, too much work, too many commitments and obligations, there isn't room to ease through a hard time. When we're squeezed, it's difficult to be creative or think about anything but our current pain. This is when we turn to things to help us to numb. It may be alcohol or other drugs, TV binges, extreme busyness, isolating, or something else that allows us to quickly turn the pain off. You don't need creative energy for that. But all that does is prolong your discomfort.

My friend, author Cyndie Spiegel, went through years of heartache. During the pandemic, she lost her nephew to senseless gun violence. Her mom died shortly after. Then her brother got very sick and was hospitalized. If all of that wasn't enough, she was diagnosed with breast cancer. Through the grief and uncertainty, she found joy. It didn't arrive only after she felt better about everything. She found it during the hardest parts. She started by creating and connecting to small things that made her smile. She called them microjoys. She wore a bright pink tulle dress in the middle of the day for no reason. She had happy hour in the front yard with lawn chairs from the '70s. She discovered that you can feel sad *and* experience joy, that you can grieve *and* laugh, and that you can be scared *and* hopeful. Likewise, you can be in pain *and* be gentle, you can make a mistake (small or big) *and* be gentle. You can be firm and direct *and* be gentle. There is no need to choose.

Speaking of mistakes, Rosamund Zander, a renowned speaker, author, and expert on leadership and personal development, has a unique recommendation for people who make mistakes: She suggests you say to yourself, "How fascinating!" In her book, *The Art of Possibility*,[2] coauthored with her husband, Benjamin Zander, she explains that this phrase can help individuals reframe their mistakes as opportunities for learning and growth, rather than sources of shame and self-criticism. This is a way to acknowledge that mistakes happen to all of us. No matter how responsible, smart, or confident we may be, we are going to mess up. The mistakes themselves aren't nearly as significant as how we respond to them. Zander suggests that if you are willing to change that response from negative self-talk and spiraling into self-doubt to saying, "How fascinating!" you can cultivate a mindset of curiosity and openness. "How fascinating!" can lead to questions like, "How might I do this differently next time?" or "What's the lesson here?" A gentler approach of wonder and curiosity can lead to motivation, inspiration, and opportunities for growth.

Zander does note that this process is not a substitute for taking responsibility for our actions. Responding to our mistakes and setbacks with "How fascinating!" is a practice in self-compassion. We can extend this compassion to others during difficult conversations. Instead of getting defensive or frustrated we can move right to curiosity with "How fascinating! Tell me more."

Usually, when we think we can't be gentle with ourselves or others, it's because we'd rather be in control. Loosening that grip to be softer might feel scary until you realize that the control you think you have is just an illusion. You actually have little control over most things with exception of your response. Will you respond from a place of pain and fear, or will you respond from a place of hope and curiosity? Will you try to control the situation, or will you be gentle?

The Tiny Steps

These tiny steps will help you begin to be gentler with yourself when you are juggling hard feelings.

- ☀ *Say, "How fascinating!"* This may sound a little silly, but putting it into practice is not only kind of fun, but it can shift your mindset from frustrated or upset to curious and interested. It takes so much pressure off the mistakes we make. So, try it. The next time you feel defensive or embarrassed, instead of coming down on yourself or shutting people out, just shrug your shoulders and say or think, "How fascinating!"

- ☀ *Identify a microjoy.* No matter how you are feeling. It can be something small that is already in your day-to-day life.

See it, experience it, and give yourself permission to enjoy it. For more microjoy examples, see in this section chapter 9's suggestions for simple pleasures and read Cyndie Spiegel's book, *Microjoys: Finding Hope (Especially) When Life Is Not Okay*.

✧ *Try it on someone else.* The next time you are in a conversation that could become contentious, say, "That's really interesting, I've never thought about it quite like this. I'll give it some thought!" For instance, when sitting at dinner with the relative who always wants to stir things up, instead of getting defensive, see what happens if you shift the conversation with this statement. Your curiosity will remove your defensiveness and perhaps make them more open to a gentler approach. If that doesn't happen, hold your boundaries about what you will or won't discuss or accept in terms of treatment from others.

One Gentle Step

If you are not up for the tiny steps today, try one gentle step. Make a quick list (on paper or in your head) of everything you are feeling right now. Put a name to your feelings even if they are scattered. Then simply write or think, "How fascinating!" and see what comes up.

Permission Slip:

I am allowed to respond from a place of hope and curiosity even when I'm in pain.

THREE

Don't Take It Personally

Caring less about what other people think is a powerful self-care practice. I know it's hard to believe, but, generally, what people think of you has nothing to do with you. It's about them. It's about what they had for breakfast, a criticism they received years ago that you somehow reminded them of, or all the messages that they hold inside.

When I first started dressing with less, one of the things that worried me was what other people would think. I worked in advertising sales and between in-office interactions, client meetings, and community events, I knew I'd be outfit repeating. How would I explain this secret project of mine? Interestingly, no one noticed. How fascinating, right?! This was a big "aha" moment for me. *Wow! I'm not the center of attention.* I thought, *If people aren't paying as close attention to me as I thought, and they aren't noticing what I wear, maybe they don't really notice what I do, either.*

That gave me quite a bit of freedom. Sometimes, people did notice or did have something to say about changes I was making in my life or about my decisions or the choices I was making. Before internalizing their feedback, I wondered if it was about me at all. When I think about what someone else is doing, it's from my own point of reference. I filter my thoughts through my past experiences, my value system, and my own preferences. If someone says to me, "I love oatmeal raisin cookies," my stomach turns and there is no way my face doesn't express, *Eww, gross*. But really, that has nothing to do with the person who thinks raisins are enjoyable. And even if I still think something is wrong with them for making that choice, they shouldn't take it personally. In this case, it's all about me (and my raisin aversion).

Like most of us, I grew up trying to please my parents and teachers by doing my best, by being good and working to meet my potential and grow into the best version of myself. It's no wonder I carried that into adulthood, treating my flaws and imperfections as a personal failure. I have failed to be good and do my best many times. Every one of those times, I thought that relaxing on the couch instead of meeting my potential had to be a character flaw. I kept these failures to myself until one afternoon in my late forties. I was crying to my therapist about how I try to be good and asking, "Why isn't it enough?!" I was expecting her to give me advice on how to be better. I wanted the bullet points, homework, something I could take productive action on! Instead she said, "What's so great about being good?" Cue a long, overdue exhale.

An X (formerly known as Twitter) post I saw, by Sierra Chas (@SierraChas), reinforced my therapist's message to stress less about "good" and "best." It says, "Go be your favorite self. We are used to 'higher' or 'best.' But 'favorite' leaves room for grace. I'm going to be the version of myself that I like right now at this moment." It had never occurred to me to be my favorite self. That would have meant my opinion of who I am mattered more than everyone else's thoughts about me. Join me in leaving this compulsion to "be good" in the past where it belongs. What's so great about being good? Giving yourself permission to be your favorite version of you will allow you to grow and give in ways that serve everyone, including you.

I've noticed that the feedback we give says so much more about us than the feedback we receive. What we say and how we say it is almost never about someone else, it's about us. That's the personal part. On the flip side, if you give me feedback, I won't take it personally. I'll listen and be curious about it. But I'll also assume that you put that feedback through your own filters and that you are just as much telling me something about you as you are about me. It's when we take things that other people say about us too personally that we either end up in tears or worse, changing the course of our lives based on something that might have had nothing to do with us. This doesn't mean we can't learn from others, only that we have to pay attention to the way feedback is delivered and, more important, how we receive it.

We also have the choice not to receive the feedback at all. Influencer and comedian Elyse Myers[1] shared a story online about when she worked as a receptionist in a hotel. She was dealing with a guest who was outraged because Elyse wouldn't let him check in twelve hours early, nor would she upgrade him to the nicest room in the hotel, even though he demanded it. He slapped his credit card down on the counter, slid it toward her, and said, "Make it happen, bitch." She calmly slid his credit card back to him and said, "I do not receive that," then walked away. Refuse to receive what is not for you, too.

Women get more feedback, compared to men, especially the unsolicited kind. One reason for this might be that historically, we take more shit because people assume we will receive it. Let's not. Being gentle doesn't mean we are willing to get walked all over. We can be the gentlest version of ourselves and still say, "No thanks, I do not receive that." Elyse didn't throw the credit card in the guest's face. She didn't argue or fight. She said five words and walked away. But she wasn't gentle for him. She was gentle for her.

It's harder to rise when everything feels like a personal attack. If the opinions of others feel untrue to you, trust yourself. Just like you have to build trust in other relationships, you also have to build trust in the relationship you have with the Gentle You. If you are second-guessing, see if there is something helpful you can extract from the overall message. For instance, if you told me you wished this book was shorter, I wouldn't be devastated or consider publishing a shorter version of the book. However, I might think about how to share something more bite-sized on my blog or social media. I tend to think of feedback not as good or bad but as useful or not. Even if it's not 100 percent useful, perhaps I can use 10 percent.

You may notice that the kind of feedback you get from some people in your life is generally supportive while feedback from others may lean more negative. This is especially not about you. It's about who they are. It may be easier to find something helpful in what these people have to offer by remembering that this is their signature delivery. The packaging isn't always great, but maybe the content is worth considering. Of course, this doesn't apply to everyone. If someone gives you feedback in an abusive way, you don't have to accommodate the delivery. It's also important not to take things personally from people who don't personally know you, starting with strangers on the internet leaving anonymous comments about who you are, what you do, or how you think.

People may have thoughts about the way you rise. Take the helpful bits and let the rest gently slip away. Don't spend your time and energy trying to decipher hidden messages or wondering what the way someone said something means. Don't fight it, don't correct it, don't wonder about it. Simply walk away, even metaphorically. You need that time and energy for the rising. If trusting what you know is true to you feels selfish, good. As author Glennon Doyle says, "We do not need more selfless women. What we need right now is more women who have detoxed themselves so completely from the world's expectations that they are full of nothing but themselves. What we need are women who are full of themselves. A woman who is full of herself knows and trusts herself enough to say and do what must be done."[2]

The Tiny Steps

Use these tiny steps to reconsider how you accept feedback and how you offer it. We all deserve room to rise by caring a little bit less about what other people think.

- *Start with a stranger.* A shift like this will require some practice. Not taking things personally and caring less about what others think goes for people you work with, strangers on the internet, and the people you love the most. That said, choosing to not receive feedback from a stranger on the internet will be easier than doing so from someone close to you. Practice with a stranger on the internet who posts something you don't agree with. Try not responding at all, or if you do, keep it neutral with something like, "Thank you for your thoughtful feedback." Then try not receiving unhelpful feedback from a client or coworker. Instead of a big response, try saying something like, "OK" or "I'll think about that." When it comes to those close to you, you can still love them while not taking what they say personally. You can still love them while saying (or thinking), "I do not receive that."

❧ *Notice the feedback you give to yourself.* Be aware of how you speak to yourself. How does it shift when you are in a good mood? A bad mood? Is your internal tone of voice different when you are hungry or anxious? Let it be a reminder of where others are coming from and when it may be best not to offer an opinion.

❧ *Make a list of things that aren't personal.* What will you not take personally anymore? If someone doesn't like your shoes, is that personal? What about your food choices? Note the things that don't matter at all so when they come up, you don't have to even consider taking it personally. Choosing in advance to let some things immediately bounce off you is a great feeling, and it will save you a lot of time torturing yourself over meaningless things people say to you. You have more important things to do.

One Gentle Step

If you are not up for the tiny steps today, try one gentle step. The next time you are in a situation where you aren't ready to speak the words, say them quietly to yourself, "I do not receive that." It's OK to practice on the inside, too.

Permission Slip:

I won't take things personally because they're probably not about me.

FOUR

Go Slowly

Remember when we talked about honoring your personal time and energy availability? Speed is an essential part of that. If you notice that you usually rush, it's time to give yourself permission to go slowly.

I get to practice going slowly every forty days or so when I'm recovering from the treatment I have for multiple sclerosis. On the day of my treatment, I head to my local infusion center. I bring my favorite things like a soft blanket, decadent hand lotion, cuticle oil, a bottle of water, and snacks. I watch a show on my computer, something that doesn't require my full attention (I'm looking at you, reality TV). I feel grateful that I can rest and heal like this. On the day after my infusion, I could push through and work, but I've learned that this is not a gentle choice for me. Because I don't always feel my best, the work that I get done is poor, and I often make myself even more tired during the following days. Now, the only thing on my schedule the day after an infusion is taking care. Instead of proving how strong I am by showing everyone that I'm back to work, I remind myself that my strength lies in my softness. Every once in a while, I wake up on the day after my treatment feeling great. Those bonus days are such a gift.

Years ago, I met a woman at an event where I had shared my story about simplifying, slowing down, getting rid of stress, and doing less to live well with MS. This woman had MS, too. She asked me, "Why aren't you afraid?" In that moment, I knew that what she really meant was, "I'm afraid." So I asked her, "Tell me more." She said, "I can't slow down and do less. In fact, since my diagnosis, I'm always in a hurry. Everything is a rush. I'm scared that soon I won't be healthy enough to do what I have to get done. So I'm pushing to get it done now, before I get too sick." As if that happening were a foregone conclusion. I explained to her that my approach was the opposite. I knew if I didn't slow down and take care that getting sicker *would* be a foregone conclusion.

Our conversation made me wonder if that's why we are all in such a hurry. Are we afraid that if we don't rush, we'll miss something, drop the ball, fall behind, run out of time and energy? Logically, we know the opposite is happening. When we hurry, we miss more, drop more, and fall further behind, as we exhaust ourselves trying to keep up. When I get caught up in hurrying, or I'm rushing around doing too much or trying to get it all done, I feel exhausted and run-down. Additionally, I make more mistakes when I rush. So, for me, to live well with MS (or really, just to live well at *all*), these things are true:

- Consistency is more important than intensity.
- Easing through works better than powering through.
- When my body says rest, I rest.
- Going slowly gets me further than rushing.

BE INTENTIONAL ABOUT YOUR SLOWDOWN

There are many ways to slow down. You can use your body to slow down by taking a little extra time before getting out of bed in the morning, to uncurl your toes and relax your jaw. Then you might raise your eyebrows a few times or shrug your shoulders. Who needs a yoga mat or gym membership to stretch out when you have your bed? Use your mind to slow down by removing yourself from drama and releasing your worries for a little while: Set a timer for five to twenty minutes (more if you have it) and divert your attention toward a creative project, writing a note to someone you love, or making a simple meal plan for next week. Breaking free of our digital devices welcomes a nice slowdown, as you'll know if you've tried a digital detox.

You can slow down by slowing your environment, too. What's around you? A cluttered space filled with lots of undone projects may feel busy and make you feel rushed on the inside. Do your surroundings demand your attention or let you be? Light a candle, find your favorite blanket, wear your coziest clothes, and slow your surroundings. Next, slow down by doing things that impede your need for speed. Anything from knitting, or petting a cat or a dog, to looking at the stars, counting backward, or saying something really sweet to yourself will do the trick.

DON'T GIVE YOUR ALL

Once again, I'm inspired by a meme. I saw a screenshot of a tweet by Sierra Wells (@sierranwells)[1] that said, "Remember that the other side of giving your all is being empty. And if you continue to give your all, you'll continue to be empty. Giving your all is unregulated and has no boundaries." I do not give my all because I refuse to leave myself with nothing. I used to commit my all to jobs, people, projects, and other things. This wasn't slow or soft. In every attempt to give my all, I'd lose it all. I deserve the love, time, and attention that the world demands of us. So do you. It's time to declutter the idea of giving your all. We are so conditioned to do our best and give it our all that we've forgotten a few important things:

1. Your best is dynamic. Your best is different at 8:00 a.m. than it is at 8:00 p.m. Your best is different before and after coffee, taking a walk, or lying down for a bit. Your best is different after you get bad news, have a fight with a friend, or spend any amount of time reading comments on the internet. It's almost impossible to measure "best," so trying to achieve it usually turns into giving too much.

2. Offering your all is unreasonable. No one should expect all of you (in your work life or your personal life), nor should you feel compelled to offer it.

3. Your best is specific to your skills and ability. Were I to give my best at removing someone's appendix or cooking in a Michelin Star kitchen, it wouldn't be very good at all. Even if I tried really hard and gave it my all, it wouldn't matter. There are some things where your best will never be enough. Let other people do those things.

4. "Do your best" and "give your all" are just different ways of saying, "Be a good girl." By doing your best and giving your all, you'll get validation and approval. And then what? You'll get to do more and give even more of yourself? Is that what you want?

Today, declutter the words and the effort behind doing your best and giving it your all. Instead, offer what you can reasonably do while taking care of yourself. Always remember: There is plenty of opportunity between giving it your all and giving it nothing to offer something meaningful and worthwhile. Now is the time to reclaim a portion of that *all* you've been giving away. It's time to say, *"I am worthy of the time, energy, and attention the world has demanded of me."* It's time to slow down and find strength in your softness, fierceness in your flexibility, and to finally rise. Not by overdoing it but by connecting with the Gentle You, standing in your light, and honoring the person you are. Celebrate you.

The Tiny Steps

If you are used to rushing through the day, these tiny steps will help you practice slowing down.

- ☘ *Underschedule.* If you never feel like you have enough time, chances are you are scheduling yourself too thin. Begin to schedule less overall and assign at least one day a week where you don't have any appointments or errands. If it feels uncomfortable, you are doing it right.

- ☘ *Schedule nothing.* If you have trouble taking time for yourself or leaving empty space on your calendar, schedule a block of nothing so you can decide what you want to do or not do in the moment on a regular basis.

- ☘ *Give a little less.* Consider the way you give your time and energy away. Do you overdo it? Give your all? One hundred and ten percent? Do your best? Stop it. To start, dial back your efforts by just 5 percent. Then try 10 percent. Save some for you. See if anyone notices. I'm almost certain that they won't.

One Gentle Step

If you are not up for the tiny steps today, try one gentle step. When your day feels overwhelming or you notice your pace is unsustainable (meaning you'll be completely worn out at the end of the day), repeat the word "slow" as a mantra and reminder to schedule things a little differently tomorrow or to let a few things go.

Permission Slip:

I will go slowly today.

FIVE

Cultivate Quiet

I t is often said that in order to be heard, we must speak up, but the truth is that speaking softly is a strength. In a noisy world, gentle words rise. I'm a person who requires lots of quiet time. I adore being around people I love, but then I need them all to go away. It's in quiet times that I tap into my strengths. This is when I rest and renew. When I come out of the quiet, I can think more clearly and be more thoughtful about creating, listening, connecting, and loving.

We need a break from the noise. Our strengths are born and nurtured in the quiet. Our softness thrives in stillness. The Gentle You craves quiet. This is true for most of the introverts I know and many extroverts as well. Even if you are very outgoing and fueled by human interaction, you still need a place to settle, listen, rest, and love. The noise we need to distance ourselves from includes the people around us, the environment we live in, the phones we depend on, our TVs, and other media. It's everywhere. The world is noisy. We can't wait for life to be quiet. We have to cultivate quiet.

I remember meeting Ashley on a group call for a simplicity immersion program. She barely spoke. She was exhausted. As she let her tears fall, she explained, "I'm sick, I'm recovering from

195

COVID. Still, I'm pushing through. But I feel overwhelmed and exhausted. On top of all of this, my husband's family loves to get together and hang out. I'm so tired, but I feel like not going isn't an option. After all, this is family!" At the pace Ashley was going, she was depleted, and it seemed likely that an even bigger crash was coming. She was standing on the edge of her cliff. I invited her to put herself in time-out. I suggested, "Why don't you try saying 'no more' to more for at least two weeks? Do what's essential and drop the rest. Including family gatherings."

Ashley took my advice. She started staying home. She got quiet, healed, and realized that the quiet was what had been missing from her life for a long time. She wanted it back. She craved the space to cultivate that quiet. She also realized that, while her husband's family was fueled by being with each other and having fun, too much family fun wore her out. No one was doing it wrong. She realized it was OK to want something different for herself. It didn't mean she didn't love her family. She just needed regular time-outs.

I could have suggested that Ashley bring a book to the next family event and make some time for herself at the gathering or to have a conversation with her family about what might work best for her, but something more immediate with a guarantee of quiet seemed appropriate. Adult time-outs are underrated. Eight weeks later, on our last small-group call, I barely recognized Ashley. By cultivating quiet, not only did she feel better, she also had a clear vision of the life she craved.

OTHER WAYS TO CULTIVATE QUIET

Quiet perfectionism. Do you struggle with perfectionism? Do you often look more closely at what you did wrong versus what you did right? Simplify your day and be gentle with yourself. Treat yourself like you would treat a good friend. Celebrate your progress (even if it's small progress) and resist the urge to pick apart all the things you could have done better.

Quiet your pace. Whenever you need to, use the power of a pause to quiet your pace, slow your thoughts and reactions, and make a little room. You can pause in conversation, pause when you are hurt, pause before you "add to cart." You can pause anytime you want to remove the momentum of stress, overwhelm, and the typical hurried pace of life.

Quiet your next walk. We are constantly entertained. When you're on a walk, the option to listen to something, from having a phone conversation to listening to a podcast or an audiobook, is always there. Instead of walking quietly, noticing our surroundings, we often fill up on outside noise. I'm not saying that this kind of noise isn't healthy or good, but do we have to always be taking it in? Walking meditation is a Buddhist practice. In a *Tricycle* magazine article,[1] Buddhist monk and peace activist Thich Nhat Hanh explains, "You don't need to make any effort at all. Your foot touches the earth mindfully, and you arrive firmly in the here and the now. And suddenly you are free—free from all projects, all worries, all expectations. You are fully present, fully alive, and you are touching the earth." While there are more formal forms of walking meditation, essentially, it's a practice in walking mindfully. You can experiment by walking slowly and noticing how your feet feel as they touch the ground, or try a brisker walk connected to your breath. You may want to start by simply walking in silence. It might be uncomfortable at first, but try and relax into it. Does your walk feel longer? Do you feel better rested?

SPEAK GENTLY

"Quiet" doesn't have to mean "silent." You could just try speaking gently. When Donna, a client from the same group program as Ashley, was telling me about a new decluttering goal she was planning to achieve, I was curious about the words she was using. She told me, "I am really demotivated and have to push through this last part." Harsh. She sounded so dejected and not excited about this project at all. I appreciate that decluttering isn't superexciting, but this sounded like she was setting herself up to be miserable. Not great for the progress she was trying to make in simplifying her life or for her mental health. I asked her, "What if, instead of buckling down, you eased in? What if instead of pushing through, you moved lightly and decluttered while gliding through your house? Or, what if you did nothing for a while and watched a movie instead?" It was clear from the nods on the Zoom screen that everyone else in our small group agreed with this. In our culture, we all use "demotivating" language, even though it does not feel good.

If you knew that your body heard every word you spoke and thought you had and responded accordingly, would you speak more gently? Would you let go of negative thoughts with more ease? Consider how you feel when someone else has a harsh word for you. It's not fun. So why do we do it to ourselves? If you want to encourage progress, speak gently instead of harshly. Almost every living thing on our planet, from plants to pets to children to grown adults, responds more favorably to a kind word over a mean one.

We can still be strong and have an impact, all while speaking gently. You don't have to take the bull by the horns, put your nose to the grindstone, get serious, or get down to business to make meaningful change.

The Tiny Steps

If you are used to rushing through the day, these tiny steps will help you practice slowing down.

❖ *Practice speaking quietly and gently.* If you feel like people aren't listening to you or giving you their attention when you raise your voice, lower it. When you find that your harsh words aren't landing well, try making them gentle. Challenge yourself to speak from the Gentle You, both to everyone around you and to yourself. How does that change each interaction? How does it shift your nervous system? When you forget, instead of giving up on it, soothe yourself with a few gentle words.

❖ *Notice the noise.* Listen to the sounds around you. What's noisy and distracting? Make a list. Include the good noise like birds singing outside of your window and the annoying noise like traffic, the internet, your phone notifications, and so on. As you slow down and notice the noises around you more and more, you will naturally gravitate to those that quiet your mind and soothe your heart.

❖ *Create quiet times and spaces.* Schedule some quiet time. Go somewhere for a bit (this will be different for everyone). This may be five minutes in your bathroom or a weekend away. Most likely, it's something in between. Choose a few places where you love to be alone and recharge. Identify a few emergency getaway spots, too. For instance, you may love to sit on a park bench and read for the afternoon— but if you only have a few minutes, a closet or bathroom may be the perfect place for a few deep breaths. Your quiet space may not be a location but an activity, like knitting, writing, or hiking. These are sacred places to go and fill your heart. Shut down your phone, turn the volume of the world down, and get quiet.

One Gentle Step

If there's too much noise for the tiny steps, try one gentle step. Create sixty seconds of as-quiet-as-possible time. Knit or enjoy a tea with noise-canceling earplugs or headphones if you have them. Get outside, put your head under the covers, close your eyes, and exhale with a "Shhhhhhhhh"... whatever it takes for a moment of quiet.

Permission Slip:

I am allowed to rest and renew by cultivating quiet, embracing quiet, and being quiet.

SIX

Dive In

You are prepared to rise—to go out into the world and take action. Yet you can't do everything at once. Everything can't matter at the same time. It can't all have your attention. Seth Godin has said that of every one thousand words we write, only ten will get attention. In this book so far, I've already written more than sixty thousand words. Are you still reading? If you notice that you've been skimming this book, email, blog articles, social media, or other things in your life, consider what might not have made it into your life, into your brain, and into your heart because there is just too much going on (inside and out). Even if I spend only five minutes on Instagram, I walk away with no idea of what just happened. Did I learn anything? Did I enjoy myself? There's no way to tell because—in just five minutes—I took in too much and my brain said, "I can't."

If you are curious about what could come from giving one area of your life more focus and attention, experiment with one of the seven suggestions below. Feed the area you choose every single day with tiny steps and commit to giving it more of your time and attention. Work on one at a time or choose something else that is important to you.

1. CONSIDER YOUR HEALTH

I probably don't have to tell you that when you feel well, things seem easier. When you don't, it's harder, it's more frustrating, and it continues to wear you down. "Health" here includes mental and physical wellness. Neither is more important than the other. If you want more focus, start by feeling better. This usually begins by you prioritizing rest. Whether you are struggling with burnout, overwhelm, or chronic illness, resting can help.

2. DECLUTTER YOUR SPACE

While decluttering often feels like the most overwhelming step on a simplicity journey, it quite literally removes obstacles and clears the path for you to simplify further. Even the little things add up. These are the items that usually matter the least, but they still get your energy and attention. Remove the things that remove you from your life.

3. CHANGE YOUR WORK

If you are like many people I know, the most stressful thing about your life right now may be your work. Sometimes it may feel easier to ignore it because it just feels impossible to change. Take it from someone who did that for years: Once a change in work becomes your primary objective, it's usually possible to achieve your goal. It may take time but as soon as you begin to imagine a new path, you can begin to see your current work situation as a means to an end—a necessary step on the journey to making changes. And sometimes just that mindset shift makes all the difference. When I say "Change your work," I don't necessarily mean "Quit your job."

Often, you can work to shift your experience inside the same job and go from hating it to feeling happier with it.

4. STOP CHECKING EMAIL

Sometimes, it seems like all we do is manage our inboxes. I recommend removing email from your phone if possible. Instead of checking it all day long, open your inbox one to three times a day. When you do, try what I suggested in section two, chapter 9, page 144, and click "select all," and then, at a glance, unselect anything you want to keep. Delete the rest. This will save you so much time and energy. If you are starting with hundreds or thousands of emails, you can try this approach and spend a few minutes each day on the older emails. Or you can declare email bankruptcy: "Select all," then delete.

5. CLEAN YOUR CLOSET

It sounds like a simple recommendation, but I know it's not. Until I cleaned out my closet and downsized my wardrobe, I had no idea the stress that was caused by my shopping for clothes, collecting wardrobe items, storing, and saving clothes and thinking about what was in my closet. The decisions around what to wear seemed endless and overwhelming. If you feel the same way, try my minimalist fashion challenge Project 333 for three months.

6. BE CONTENT

When you don't like what you do, what you have, or who you spend time with, focus becomes increasingly challenging. While a change may be in order, a hard stop may not be an option. In the meantime, be grateful. Every day, make a tiny list of things that make you smile and warm your heart. Even when life is bad, there is always something that deserves your gratitude. Prioritize simple pleasures. Do something you love. Add something lovely to your life while you try to figure stuff out. Try a photography class, bake cookies, read a book, or go for a bike ride. Even while you are struggling with discontent, write your own prescription for happiness.

7. GET PRESENT

If overwhelm, fear, and worry prevent you from showing up for your life, get present. When we are overwhelmed, fear and worry hang out and distract us from focusing on one thing. While we are trying to accomplish that one little thing, we worry about everything else that's been left undone. We start to fear that we will never accomplish anything. Which makes it hard to make any progress. This is a result of future-thinking and can be remedied by staying in the moment. If that whole idea seems completely foreign to you, set a timer for twenty minutes and commit to the task at hand, while asking your fear and worry to wait. You can even say out loud, "Hey worry, I promise I'll get back to you as soon as the timer is done!" If twenty minutes is too long, try ten. When the timer rings you can get back to fear and worry. If it feels essential to you, it will still be there. Practice increasing the time you focus on being in the moment by a little bit each day. It's kind of like the Zen kōan, "Before enlightenment, chop wood, carry water. After enlightenment, chop wood, carry water." Of course, your "chopping wood" might be doing dishes and your "water carrying" might be picking up groceries or making dinner.

FIND YOUR FOCUS BY NOTICING
WHERE YOU LOST IT

You know that thing people say when you've lost something: "Where is the last place you had it?" Honestly, I always find it annoying. If I knew that, I wouldn't have lost it! But...it does remind me to retrace my steps, so I'm more likely to find what I lost. If you've lost your focus and ability to stay engaged in what matters to you, ask yourself, *Where is the last place I had it?* When did it slip away? When you have too much to do or too many ideas to choose from, it's hard to determine what comes first. By asking yourself the question, *What was I doing when I lost focus?* you can remember what you were working on before you got pulled into something else. Then, you can get back to it; most likely, the original task you were doing is the one that deserves your attention. When you can get clear on what actually deserves your attention, as opposed to simply demanding it, you will find focus. When something distracts you or pulls you away, ask yourself, *Is this deserving of my attention or just demanding it?* and then act accordingly.

I don't know about you, but I don't want to skim through my life, manage a zillion surface-level relationships, or try to work the exhausting way everyone else is working. Instead, I want to unsubscribe from the status quo. I want simpler, slower, softer. I want long stretches of time to daydream, to be creative, to connect or disconnect. I'm aware of how privilege, different life stages, and time and energy availability factor in here; you can't always abandon your day-to-day responsibilities so you can clean out your closet, write a book, or fulfill your lifelong dream. You can, however, become more discerning about what's important to you, cut out what isn't serving you, and give as much extra attention as you have to at least one thing that matters.

Skimming doesn't serve you. It distracts you.

Choose deeper over wider. Immerse yourself in what matters to you.

Get lost in what you care about. That's where you'll find everything you've been looking for.

The Tiny Steps

Feeling too scattered and unfocused to decide what to do next? These tiny steps will help.

- ✳ *Get lost.* Make time to get lost in one thing you care about. I really cared about writing this book. While I wrote some of it during my regular work hours, I wrote most in dedicated spurts where nothing else happened but coffee, food, sleep, and walks. When I didn't have a few days to dive in, I wrote in the early morning. During those times, I let myself get lost in the work. What a gift.

- ✳ *Set a timer.* Limit your time around the things that aren't important to you. Next time you have the urge to read, scroll, or engage with information you don't really care about, see what happens when you do it for only five minutes. Could you retain the information you took in? Did it feel overwhelming? Do you need to give that activity more time? Or less?

- ✳ *Chop wood, carry water.* Assign the intention of "chopping wood and carrying water" to one or two of your daily tasks. When you're doing them, be extra present, even if your normal tendency is to multitask your way through. Does showing all the way up for washing dishes, picking up the kids from school, or folding laundry calm your brain?

One Gentle Step

If you are going in too many directions today, try the gentle step. Simply stop. Set a five-minute timer and stare out the window or at the wall, or close your eyes. Don't take anything else in for at least five minutes.

Permission Slip:

Not everything needs my attention. Most things don't.

SEVEN

Release Every Worry

When I began to share my MS diagnosis, I got a lot of advice (most of it unsolicited, of course). I heard everything from, "You probably have Lyme disease." To "It's a good idea to remodel your home or move to another, so that when you are in a wheelchair you can get around more easily." And so, I worried. I worried about falling off the cliff, like my doctor told me I might if didn't take care of myself. I worried that I'd wake up blind. I worried that I wouldn't be able to feel my feet hit the floor when I got out of bed. I also worried that I wouldn't be able to take care of my daughter. The worst part of the worrying was that everything I worried about became a little movie playing on a loop in my mind. I could see myself moving through my life, unable to function anymore. When I closed my eyes and dissolved into worry, I saw my daughter crying because I couldn't bring her to school or make her dinner. None of these movies ended with world-changing solutions, only despair and stress. We all know how despair and stress makes us feel. This is how we literally worry ourselves sick.

Generally, worries are completely made-up stories we tell ourselves about something that hasn't happened yet. But even though we know it hasn't happened, our bodies absorb our feelings about the worries as if they were happening right now. Any of us who've lain in bed and watched one of our own worry movies will have experienced this. All of that fear, angst, and stress wraps around our bones. If worry helped us take action and solve problems, maybe it would be worth it. But does it ever? In my experience, worry interrupts our sleep, our work, the way we connect with each other, and more. Worry keeps us up at night, weighs us down in the day, and makes us tired, cranky, and scared. It doesn't fix anything. Worry is a trap.

Getting out of the worry trap doesn't mean we'll never worry. We just won't stay for the whole movie. Instead, we'll find ways to release worries without having to experience all of those negative emotions squeezing our bones and our heart. When we are paralyzed with worry, it's harder to rise. When we realize that the way something turns out never depends on how much we've worried about it, we can work to release those worries and take a step forward. I'm going to suggest some gentle strategies, but before I do: If you are a chronic worrier or if you are worried about something very big (even though you still know it's out of your control), give yourself lots of grace—some of these strategies may take time. Equally, if you have anxiety that is related to trauma, letting go of your worries with these methods may be a lot more challenging. As with everything in this book, consider applying what's useful and leave the rest. Here are nine gentle strategies to help you release worry:

1. BE PRESENT

Worry is always about the past or the future. It's never about now. When you see your worry movie begin to play, come back to the present moment. Look around, notice the feeling of your feet on the ground. If you are in bed, sit up for a moment, wiggle your toes, and blink your eyes. It usually only takes a small movement to come back. If you need more, notice anything you can see, hear, or smell. The more you practice being present, the easier it gets to become present.

2. WRITE OUT THE WORRY

When you worry, you can spin it around in your brain, ruminate, and get all caught up in the movie. Or you can write it down. Make a quick list. Or write it out, scene by scene. When you can see the worry on paper, it isn't as mysterious anymore. If the worry doesn't feel specific, try and name it. What is really bothering you? If you aren't sure, review your day, step by step, from the beginning. Was anything upsetting? Is anything coming up in the near future that has you rattled? Write about it, including what it is and what the worst-case scenario might be. Get it off your mind and onto paper. If you don't like to write, make a quick audio recording about your worry. When you're finished, listen to it and then ceremoniously delete it. Goodbye, worry.

3. HAVE FEWER THINGS TO WORRY ABOUT

Simplicity helps you worry less. I used to worry about making ends meet, then I started working on having fewer ends. With less around, there is less worry. Be discerning about what you choose to surround yourself with. Some worries may surprise us, but by releasing every worry you can through simplicity, you may have more capacity for the unexpected. Hold on to what matters. Let go of the rest.

4. TAKE ACTION

While worry doesn't usually spark solutions, with some luck and intention you can transform a worry into action. Ask yourself what you can do about your worry besides allowing it to consume you. Make a list of ten things you can do. If there is an action you can take, take it. If there is nothing you can do, see #2.

5. HOLD ON

I know that there are some worries that won't be moved by the things I've mentioned so far. Thankfully, these worries are usually temporary, and all you have to do is hold on and try a few of the strategies below (especially #6). When you lose your footing, the Gentle You will be your ground.

6. ASK FOR HELP

If you can't see through your worry, if it's eating you up on the inside and you cannot let it go, ask someone you love for help, or find someone like a counselor or therapist you can talk to. We often shame ourselves for worrying, which makes it hard to share. But sharing diminishes the shame and the worry. It also gives you a chance to see that you aren't the only one who struggles with worrying, even about small things.

7. MOVE YOUR BODY

Take a walk. Go to a yoga class or do that stretch in bed thing we talked about in this section's chapter 4, "Go Slowly." Turn on your favorite music and dance around your house. Go for a walk to the end of your street and back. If you are under the weather or physically unable to move in these ways, find something smaller. Wiggle your toes. Look straight ahead, then up, to the left, down, and to the right. Scrunch up your face and then let it relax. Do that five more times. Literally shake off the worry by moving.

8. READ A BOOK

Sometimes all it takes to get out of the worry trap is a little distraction. Get lost in a love story or read something that transports you to a different time and place. When you can't remove your worries, remove yourself from them.

9. COME BACK TO LOVE

When you feel trapped by worry, come back to love. When you notice you are in the worry trap in your mind, back-burner the worry and think about who you love, what you love, and how you love. Be as present as possible in feeling this love until your worries begin to slip away.

You may not have the power to stop worries from showing up, but you often have the power to shift the way you think and feel. If you are stuck in the worry trap, do what you can to take the steps necessary to break free. Turn the movie off. You deserve to lay your head on your pillow at the end of the day and rest easy. You deserve to engage in ordinary moments during the day that result in laughter, new ideas, and long-lasting memories. You deserve to be free from constant worry.

The Tiny Steps

Use these tiny steps to move you out of your worried heart. If you think *I'm just a worrier* or imagine that your worry is necessary, test your stories. See if you can rise with more ease and make a difference without your worry.

- *Put a worry list next to your bed.* You know that thing that happens when you wake up in the middle of the night and feel worried? When you tell yourself you can let it go and fall asleep again, but your brain takes hold and keeps chewing and chewing on your worry? Your brain is trying to help you by keeping a list of your worries. Write them down and promise yourself that if you need to, you'll come back to them tomorrow.

- *Worry.* Set aside some worry time. Set a timer. Give yourself a few minutes or longer if needed to dedicate time to process your worries. When the timer goes off, get back to your day. Or pick a specific daily time. If you know that each day from 10:00 to 10:15 you are going to worry, your mind can leave it alone for a while. If you decide to skip worry time, that's fine, too. No worries.

- *Distract yourself.* What can you do to distract yourself from an endless cycle of worrying? Usually, it helps to give your mind something else to listen to. Call a friend and ask them about their day or listen to a podcast. I highly recommend the *Soul & Wit* podcast for something light-hearted that will probably make you laugh and forget your worries. You could also listen to an audiobook or a playlist of your favorite music. Sometimes a pause will break the loop, and the worry won't seem as important when you come back to it.

One Gentle Step

If you are worried that the tiny steps are too much today, start with one gentle step. Schedule your worry time. Instead of worrying in fits and spurts all day long, give yourself five to fifteen minutes to go all in. Set an alarm or remind yourself in another way that you'll have time to worry later. If you don't feel worried at your scheduled worry time, cancel your session and revisit tomorrow. Worry can wait.

Permission Slip:

Because I realize that how something ends up never depends on how much I worry about it, I can worry less.

EIGHT

Ask Yourself

There's this viral video with a little girl, about two years old, wearing bright red lipstick that she had clearly applied herself because it's covering more than just her mouth. In the video, her dad is behind the camera, and he asks her, "Whose lipstick is that?" She says, "It's mine." Then the dad asks her, "Did you ask anyone if you could put it on?" She replies, "I asked myself." Google "girl wearing lipstick from Home Depot" and you'll see why it inspired this chapter.[1] It's as if she's giving us all permission to take what we need for ourselves. I shared the lipstick video with the Simplicity Space Community, and their responses echoed my own:

- *Love the idea of asking myself!*
- I marveled at her self-confidence. It reminded me we all have this bravado and self-love as kids. Society, on the other hand, and trying to "fit in" so desperately makes our self-doubt rear its ugly head. I want to trust myself again.
- From now on, when making decisions, the first person I'll ask what to do is myself.
- The wisdom of babes. It's called "internal consent" and it's definitely a journey to re-attune myself to this after a lifetime of people pleasing.

I first watched that video with my sister, Alyson, in 2023. Today, if we are chatting and I tell her about something I did for myself, she'll say, "Did you ask anyone if you could do that?" I always laugh and say, "I asked myself." Or, if either of us is struggling with a decision or to give ourselves permission to do something we want, we reshare the video with each other. It always does the trick.

This is going to sound very Wizard of Oz, but we spend so much of our lives seeking approval, validation, and love from other people when, actually, it's always been within us. The Gentle You is waiting with all these gifts. But it will take a little more than clicking your heels together to connect with her. Instead of getting all dressed up in ruby slippers, I prefer to form the connection by putting my hands on my heart.

Finding little ways to reconnect with the Gentle You will help you rise every time. She'll always tell you the truth, support your thoughtful decisions, and encourage you to take the steps you know are best for you. She understands that it takes courage to rise. She can help you be brave enough, no matter what other people say or think, by reminding you of who you are and what you want, and that you have what it takes to make that a reality. It's lovely to have people like that in your life. Imagine how powerful it is to be that person for yourself. When I'm not sure which stage of Gentle I need the most, I consult the Gentle Me. I ask, "Rest, less, or rise?" When I ask, I am reminded that while I appreciate and often depend on the support of others, I know me best. I am here for me. I care about me. I believe in me. I am brave enough to rise.

AFTER YOU ASK YOURSELF, ASK OTHERS

The more that you depend on the Gentle You to figure out what is best for you—the more you trust yourself—the more doors will open for you to learn from other people. This isn't about looking for the absolute answer or putting your decisions fully in someone else's hands. Instead, the solid foundation you've created will allow you to be more receptive to new ideas, thoughts, and opinions, and to take them into thoughtful consideration without drowning out your own knowing. And the more receptive you are, the more you can expand your community purposefully—surrounding yourself with more and more people to gain wisdom from, bounce ideas off, and brainstorm with.

CREATE COMMUNITY

We all desire to be a part of something (even an introvert like me). We all long to connect with like-hearted people, and to grow and thrive with others. "Grow and thrive" might mean supporting each other's careers or trading recipes. The way you grow and thrive with others might mean getting together each month to discuss a book or to support a cause through political activism. You might volunteer with others, drink coffee with them, and even develop friendships. All of these things are born in community. By the way, you don't have to start a community to create it. You could join one that already exists. A big part of creating the community experience is just showing up.

Some communities are online, making them much more accessible. From well-supported Facebook groups to other platforms like Mighty Networks and Circle, a little searching and discerning (with the help of the Gentle You) means you may find something you enjoy. Before joining a community, ask yourself the following questions.

- What kind of community do I want to join? What am I looking for?

- How much time do I want to commit?
- How do I want to communicate with others? Live calls, text messages, online community chat, in-person meetings?

Once you start looking, you may change your mind, but going in with that clear understanding gives you some parameters to navigate something new with more ease.

The Simplicity Space is the community I started right after the pandemic began. It hit just after I had closed all my online offerings because I'd planned to be out in the world doing more live events. What's that saying about God and plans? With the level of uncertainty, fear, and grief at an all-time high, I knew it wasn't just me who was craving connection and support. The Simplicity Space community started on Facebook. Then we moved to Mighty Networks (a platform where people can read and comment on announcements and swap messages) and grew into something that felt safer, more like home, and didn't risk us "just checking" Facebook. Over the last few years members of our community have shown up for live calls, worked with me when they crave extra support, and even become friends who meet up in different states and countries.

In New York, the group City Girls Who Walk started in 2022 on TikTok when Brianna Kohn posted a TikTok inviting people to take a walk with her.[2] She was feeling lonely and craving connection. Two hundred fifty people showed up in Central Park, many women arriving alone. Now they have hundreds of people showing up for walks not only in New York but in cities around the world. Women are gathering in Los Angeles, Boston, Washington, DC, Dubai, Chicago, Lisbon, Phoenix, Detroit, Philadelphia, and Stockholm. Kohn guesses that there are City Girls Who Walk groups in close to two hundred cities. Participants say things like, "These strangers have become amazing friends with whom I can share laughter and tears, they have become the most wonderful adventure buddies I could have ever wished for."

Perhaps you'll join the Simplicity Space, start a City Girls Who Walk chapter, or join a book club. Even though you'll always continue to ask yourself, being with people who have a similar interest, hobby, or outlook on life will encourage your risings.

The Tiny Steps

Use these tiny steps to help you get clarity on what you want and need.

- *Ask yourself.* Find a way to connect with the Gentle You so you can tap into the courage, validation, confirmation, and love you seek. There isn't one right way. You may employ different strategies mentioned in this book or discover others on your own.

- *Ask others.* Connect with the wisdom around you. If you aren't sure about next steps, ask your most trusted people to weigh in. Then process their advice through the lens of the person who knows you best: you. When you aren't sure about feedback that makes you feel defensive, think, *How fascinating.* See if there is any goodness that you can extract even from negative feedback (but not abusive feedback).

- *Consider community.* What kind of people do you want to spend time with? Think about how you'd like to spend an hour a week or an hour a month with others—what activities would connect you? Make a list of five to ten communities you'd like to look into (online or in person). Search around similarities like hobbies, career, or activities you enjoy.

❖ *Start something new.* This is an important tiny step: If you can't find what you are looking for, or you have a great idea for a community to bring people together, start brainstorming. Ask the same questions you were asking when thinking about joining a community because even when you start it, you'll be a part of it, too. Then put the word out. Tell your friends, post something on social media, or just ask a couple of people you know if they'd like to join you one day (and then again, a week or a month later).

One Gentle Step

If the tiny steps feel too big today, try one gentle step. Search for "girl wearing lipstick from Home Depot" and share it with someone you love to laugh with. You may end up sending it back to each other in the future.

Permission Slip:

When I want something, before I look for permission from those around me I will simply ask myself. Permission granted!

NINE

Savor Simple Pleasures

At the very beginning of the book, I was talking about the importance of realizing you need and deserve rest without "earning" it, and I invited you to rest first. Remember? I like to think of simple pleasures the same way. What if instead of bribing yourself with simple pleasures, you enjoyed them whenever you wish? When I first began to simplify, I focused on less. Less stuff, less debt, less obligation, and less stress. I'd think about more, too, and what I wanted from this simplicity journey. I was craving better health, more savings, and more love. Recently, I've been interested in more pleasure. I don't know why I waited so long. I assume it's that whole "work hard to deserve nice things" mentality that was drilled into me by our culture. It got in my way.

Earlier, when I talked about *The Tiny Step Simplicity Challenge* that I ran, I mentioned how a few people felt frustrated because we were going too slowly. Then, at the end of the week, they were surprised by their progress. Another thing that surprised them was that their first task wasn't to declutter a junk drawer or donate a bunch of stuff. Instead, it was to enjoy a simple pleasure every single day. When I invited them to give themselves this gift, some people pushed back. They didn't see the connection between taking time to enjoy their day and making progress on habit changes...at first.

How do simple pleasures and little luxuries help us rise? How does doing something we enjoy just for the sake of enjoying it help us? It fills us with joy. When we feel joy, we remember how little we actually need to be inspired, motivated, and curious. Joy gives us space to take action with more ease. Simple pleasures are usually ordinary things, sometimes so ordinary that we forget to see them as a pleasure.

For example, my morning coffee is a whole *thing*. It's not just a cup of fuel that I grab as I'm rushing out the door to get me going—it also isn't something that happens in the middle of five hundred other tasks. Instead, it's a simple pleasure that I give the attention it deserves. I take out my favorite cup and make the coffee. Before I begin to sip, I either start some music or call Alyson (my sister). She lives in Germany, so she has her afternoon coffee while I have my morning coffee. It's a pleasure I give myself before I check anything off my to-do list. I may not have even brushed my hair before I'm indulging and filling my cup, literally and figuratively.

My other simple pleasures include walks around the neighborhood, either in silence or while listening to a podcast that makes me laugh (or something more escapist, like a story about a scam artist), journaling, and doodling. Simple pleasures aren't the things we have to do, they are things we want to do.

Your simple pleasures may include a morning beverage like tea or coffee or the citrus tonic in section 1, chapter 3. Perhaps walking while chatting with a friend in person or on the phone is a simple pleasure. Cupcakes, bubble baths, and great playlists come to mind, too. If you are having trouble identifying a simple pleasure, think about what pleases one or more of your five senses. A soft blanket can be a simple pleasure for your sense of touch. A small piece of dark chocolate may be just right for your taste buds. A spritz of your favorite perfume or lighting a scented candle will be a pleasure for your sense of smell. Looking at images from your favorite artist, reading a book, or scrolling through a museum or even your camera roll and choosing an "image of the week" may serve your sense of sight. Beautiful music or listening to the birds sing is a simple pleasure for your hearing.

Of course, as you awaken each sense with a simple pleasure, your brain and heart get involved, too. Earlier I asked you to compare what it feels like to move through the day after a great night of sleep versus a bad one. Here, imagine rising from a place of apathy or discouragement versus one where you feel joyful. Simple pleasures will help you fill your cup so you have a reservoir of joy, creativity, and love to dip into.

If you've been on a simplicity journey or are interested in minimalism, you may notice that simple pleasures aren't often part of the program/book/article that you are being inspired by. That's a disservice to you. I probably contributed to that during my early days of blogging about simplicity. Some of us alluded to it by saying things like, "Make room for what matters" or "Spark joy"; while these are both great ideas, they are giant concepts. Too giant when you are just getting started. Ideas like "joy" and "what matters" aren't often measurable and certainly not enjoyable at first. When you are simplifying or changing another habit focused only on rules, discipline, and your lack of success in the past, your cup empties quickly. Giving yourself a simple pleasure on a consistent basis is something tangible that you can enjoy immediately. It can help you to begin to define some of what "joy" means in your own life. If nothing else, simple pleasures make the journey a little sweeter.

WHY JOY (IN THE FORM OF
A SIMPLE PLEASURE) MATTERS

When you are working on a new habit change, it's easy to hyper-focus on control. In some ways, it makes logical sense to want to prioritize only what must get done. The thing is, those big special goals and changes are likely going to take more than ten minutes or even ten days. I have some that I've been working on for ten years or more. If you don't allow yourself joy until the end, as a reward for when you are done, how on earth can you expect to enjoy anything along the way?

Without simple pleasures, I'm more likely to let my connection to whatever I'm focused on slowly fizzle out. We typically assign the activities that bring us joy as rewards for working hard, meeting our goals, and sticking to our new habits. We think, *If I keep this up for ten days, then I'm going to give myself a treat.* This is what we do at work, when we push through until our vacation (in the hopes that in one or two weeks, we can somehow recover from a year's worth of hard work). A more reliable way to experience joy is, once again, to change the way you change and give yourself a simple pleasure every single day (no problem if it's the same one).

By allowing simple pleasures, microjoys, and other tiny moments that invite you to be present, you get to enjoy your life every single day. When we withhold simple pleasures in the name of getting more done, or tell ourselves other ways we don't deserve them, we suffer unnecessarily. A simple pleasure can help us reset. It can motivate us when we are making a big change. We might try and tell ourselves that we don't have time, there's too much to do, but as we've established, there will *always* be too much to do. Let's create more opportunities to enjoy, get present, and show up for our lives.

When someone asks me how to declutter faster, or change jobs, or set a boundary quickly, one of my first recommendations is always "Prioritize simple pleasures." I prioritize simple pleasures every day for myself, too. From fresh flowers on my kitchen table to lighting a favorite candle or chatting with my sister while we both drink coffee in different countries, I do things that feel good not because I've earned them, but just because they feel good.

The Tiny Steps

Use these tiny steps to prioritize simple pleasures in your day-to-day life. You don't have to save them for a special occasion or until you think you deserve them. You get to give them to yourself right now because you *are* the special occasion.

- ÷ *Put joy first.* Remember to plan your simple pleasures each day. Don't decide you'll try to fit them in later. Don't just hope they happen naturally. They won't. Prioritize them. After a while, experiencing these simple pleasures will be like brushing your teeth, something you just always do because you know it's good for you. For now, add them to your calendar, set an alarm, or do whatever it takes to make them happen.
- ÷ *Make a list of simple pleasures.* Keep a list so you don't have to spend time figuring out what brings you joy. This will be especially helpful on very busy days or when you are experiencing something hard. This way, you can just go to your list, pick a thing, and use that little slice of delight as a reminder that you can have joy, rest, and simple pleasures even while you have a mile-long to-do list. Any time. You don't have to be supercreative with your simple pleasures, either. You may repeat them every day if you want to (like

I do with my coffee). Don't forget to notice the simple pleasures that are already right in front of you. What lights you
up during the day that you may already do automatically?
From your coffee or tea to a slow morning, instead of just
getting through it, what if you savored it instead?

÷ *Understand your resistance.* If you won't allow yourself a
simple pleasure until you feel like you've earned it, if they
always show up on the bottom of your to-do list, try to
remember when you first started depriving yourself of
things you enjoy. Who told you that you can't eat dessert
first? Who said you have to earn your joy? Do you still
need to listen to that person? Maybe instead you could
take your cues from the Gentle You.

÷ *Share your simple pleasures.* Spread the idea of simple pleasures with people you want to connect with. Invite them
for a walk, share your favorite feel-good playlist, or invite
them to join you for a coffee (in person or virtual).

One Gentle Step

If the tiny steps feel too big today, try one gentle step.
Identify a simple pleasure that requires very little energy.
For instance, is there a movie or show you love that you
haven't watched in a while? Pick a favorite scene and tune
in for a few minutes.

Permission Slip:

*I will treat myself to a simple pleasure today (and savor the hell
out of it).*

TEN

Live the Life You Actually Want

I t's 2:30 on a Friday afternoon. I'm standing looking at a jewelry case of stunning (and very expensive) diamond rings, and I'm thinking, *Wow. Just . . . WOW.* I'm thirty-seven years old, working in sales and marketing, and I'm meeting with a client in their jewelry store. The store is run by two women who are just beautiful, and visually dripping with wealth. They have perfect fingernails, expensive haircuts, and, of course, the jewelry: bracelets, necklaces, and very fancy watches—I can't see the brand names, but it's clear they're Rolex or Patek Philippe. My cheeks flush when I remember that I am wearing a Swatch. When I think they aren't looking, I try to slide my blazer down and cover it. Then they point to the rings and say, "Why don't you try one on?"

At this point in my life, I'm less of a jewelry person and more someone who dreams about fancy shoes and luxury-brand clothing. I'm also so deep in debt that I'd usually never think about buying something so pricey, but being with these women in this jewelry store, looking at the sparkling rings on my fingers, I wonder if I should get more into jewelry. As they show me different pieces it feels like we're bonding. For a second, I think, *We're sharing a moment!* But then...I know they're probably thinking, *This woman could never afford our jewelry.* I visualize myself pulling out a credit card and laugh (on the inside) for considering a $5,000 purchase. At the same time, I start to wonder if owning one of those rings will help me get *there*.

There, into the life that I knew I should have had. The life that I'd have if I was the "grown-up" version of me. Grown-up Courtney would make more money than I did. She would wear nicer clothes than I did. She'd have fancier furniture, and probably a walk-in closet. I was always trying to get "there," and I couldn't get "there" with my financial situation, so I just went deeper and deeper into debt. I kept working toward this version of myself and my life by trying to prove who I was with what I had. But I kept coming up short because there was a cognitive dissonance between what I thought I wanted and what I actually wanted. What I thought I wanted was not what my heart wanted. I never felt satisfied, which meant I never felt like I was "there." I always felt behind, and like I wasn't doing it right. So to soothe myself, I'd spend more money and buy more things.

Then I got diagnosed with MS and I had to rest. It wasn't because I'd already mapped out the structure of this book. It was because I was simply too sick to do anything else. I had to surrender, I had to give up. I had to learn how to take care of myself. Once I was a little better, I started to research. I found out that stress exacerbates MS symptoms and can lead to a decline in overall health. So my goal became to remove stress. I began to let go of layers: layers of my belongings, layers of busyness, layers of expectations about my identity and around how hard I worked.

What I didn't anticipate was that I wasn't just letting go of those layers. I was letting go of who I thought I was supposed to be. I discovered that I wanted to give myself a break from meeting another goal, climbing another ladder, faking another smile. I discovered that the things that I defined myself by before—being the best salesperson, the most committed volunteer, and someone who said yes to every opportunity—didn't have to be who I am.

Seven years after my visit to the jewelry shop, it's now a Friday night, and I'm sitting on my couch being squished from either side. On my left, Wilbur, my cat, is kneading my leg. On the other side of Wilbur is Bailey, my daughter, who is seventeen and about to go off to college. She's cuddling our giant dog, Guinness, who is spread out and drooling on the chaise. On my right side is my husband, Mark, and on the other side of Mark is cat number two, Ella, sitting as far away from the dog as possible. Behind me is the kitchen island, so close that I can reach up and set our plates from the takeout we just had on the counter—I don't even have to stand up. The city is bustling beyond the balcony outside of the sliding doors, and a movie is on TV.

As I watch the movie, my chest feels like it's bursting with sunshine. I look around and I think about how only last week we were in a very different place. We were in our two-thousand-square-foot house with its four bedrooms, two bathrooms, kitchen, dining room, separate living room and family room, a big yard, a garage, and even a storage shed. Then the six of us (including the pets) moved. We were now living in a 750-square-foot apartment with a small kitchen–living room, two bedrooms, one bathroom, no private garage, no yard, and definitely no storage shed or extra space to store anything.

And I was so happy. For so long, everything I thought I needed to be an adult, to be happy, to be me, was wrong. In fact, it separated me from what I care about most. I thought the bigger my home, closet, and bank account were, the more my happiness would grow.

What I didn't know then was that in a smaller home, I would find so much more space. I would find a level of contentment I hadn't even known was possible. What I discovered was that in this slower, softer life I didn't have to be hurried or overwhelmed with belongings and extra commitments. Instead of spending every day checking off goals and obligations, I had room to enjoy and connect, to rest and rise. My life became less of a checklist and more like a movie I wanted to watch again and again. Finally, I was able to actually be in my life and be present for it. Looking around this room, squashed on the couch with suddenly so few belongings, I realize all I can see is all I care about. It feels whole. It feels complete. It feels gentle. I understand that I can have this feeling anytime I want, and I don't need anything from outside of myself to get it.

We've all daydreamed about the life we'd like to have. Most likely, we've daydreamed about several different kinds of life; as they tend to, cravings change over time. We've also all dismissed those lives we crave. We've ignored the pulls to change our habits, simplify, and make room for our hearts. To-do lists, societal pressure, broken systems, exhaustion, and frustration all get in the way.

Now, you have a solution. Using the steps in this book that resonate with you, you have a way to fulfill some of those daydreams by making time and space to show up for your life and align with the Gentle You. Once you connect with the Gentle You, and continue to strengthen that connection, you can trust it with every fiber of your being. You'll begin to create moments that will result in the life you crave.

Be open to the shifting nature of what you want for your life. On some days you may crave a small life, and on other days you may want a big one. Or, you may want a big little life—whatever that means to you. Trying to define and commit to a life in one particular shape is not the path for most of us.

Over the last ten years, there were times when I wanted to sell everything and travel the world, then others when I rarely wanted to leave the comforts of home. I do know that after getting rid of most of the things that held me back, I find great delight in recognizing my cravings for life. I experience even more joy when I get what I'm looking for in one single moment, without having to turn everything upside down. I reach these points when the changes that happened on the inside are more important than the ones on the outside.

It's also glorious to want something for yourself just because you want it and not for anyone else's approval or benefit. It's a feeling of contentment and satisfaction that cannot be replicated by trying to measure up, catch up, or be some version of yourself that appeals to everyone (but you). Consider that the life you actually want isn't usually driven by what you are doing. It's about how you feel and who you are, how you move through the world.

Li, a member of the Simplicity Space, once asked me for help. She said, "I want to create a daily meditation habit. For some reason I struggle being consistent. Nothing has worked except physically going to classes, which I can't prioritize right now. I tried only meditating for a few minutes a day but even that hasn't worked. Any other clever ideas?" I gave her two. The first was to try an app like Headspace that offers guided meditation, including those one-minute meditations I mentioned in the introduction. Then I suggested, "Consider why you want to meditate. What do you want to feel or gain from meditating?" Based on what she'd shared so far, it didn't sound like she wanted to meditate at all. I asked her, "Can you identify what you really want from meditation? Is there maybe something else that would get you there without the struggle of trying to meditate?"

Often, the thing we think we want to do is not the thing we actually want to do. It's often not even the thing we have to do in order to feel how we want to feel. When I am craving something for my life, I usually find myself cooking up a complicated ten-part plan behind the scenes. Instead of jumping into it, I pull back and ask, "What do I really want?" What I'm looking for here isn't more work, it isn't more striving, proving, and doing. When it's time to rise, I ask why. Where do I want to be? Usually, I want to feel a certain way. So then, I reverse engineer, figure out how to get *there* and look for ease, for the Gentle Way. Maybe one day I will always automatically start gently. In the meantime, it usually takes me a little unlearning, loosening my grip, and remembering how good it feels to create, grow, and love gently.

When you feel unsettled with where you are, when it's time to change something about your life—to rise—remember: Once upon a time, the life you have now may have been what you craved back then. This isn't to say that things should stay the same, but connecting with some level of appreciation for what you've already created may help you see your life in a different light. Even if it is time to let go of something, gratitude for how you got it could make you feel happier or more at ease during the transition.

Before you shut down your next craving, goal, or dream because it feels too impossible, open up. Love yourself through the craving, goal, or dream. Get lost in the possibility. How would you feel if you got what it was you most wanted? If achieving this particular dream genuinely feels impossible, first, decide if that is for sure the reality of the situation. Then, if it is, get curious about what else you could do to feel that way. Or is the issue just the timing? Perhaps it's time to rest. Make sure the voice telling you, "This is impossible" isn't your mean elementary school teacher, a bad boss, or the awful ex who told you you'd never make it on your own. Ask yourself. Ask the Gentle You. Let that voice be the loudest. Let that voice be the truth.

Combined, the seasons of *Gentle* will help you live the life you want. They will help you redefine where "there" is for you. Each stage of this book also exists just for the sake of itself. Be in the stage of Rest to be rested. Embrace Less so you can create space, time, and energy. Rise to make a difference in your world and in the world. Use each stage to get closer to the Gentle You. Every section, chapter, and tiny step is an invitation and a practice to stay connected to the Gentle You.

In every one of my books, I've written the following words, and they still hold true: *If you want to be light, you have to let go.* Stop sacrificing the life you want for regret, resentment, anger, and maintaining a tough exterior. Don't miss the life you want to live in the name of being a grown-up or doing what you think grown-ups are supposed to do—*you* make the rules. Being gentle, soft, flexible, and quiet isn't a weakness—it's a strength. The Gentle You is always in your corner, always rooting for you, supporting you, and standing with you.

When you feel lost or overwhelmed, or you aren't sure about next steps, remember...

Be Gentle.
Move softly.
Go slowly.
Celebrate every tiny step.

You don't have to push through.
Ease through.
Be light.
Be you.

I am writing this book at the end of the year. Like every year, there were highs and lows. There were even more in-betweens. That is where the magic lives. It's in those little moments. Like this one I'm in the middle of right now. The sun isn't up yet, the house is quiet, and I'm fully aware that in this in-between, nothing-special moment is a slice of the life I crave. I'm living it, one moment at a time. As I write this paragraph, I don't know what the next year or even the next day holds for your life or for mine. We never really know what's next. We resist uncertainty, but it's deeply woven into being human. I feel content with that lack of knowing. I know the feeling is fleeting. But I'm not worried. While it's impossible to preserve this tiny moment of peace and ease I'm feeling right now, I know that Gentle is always here for me, for us. The Gentle You, the Gentle Me, the Gentle Us.

Acknowledgments

Thank you for reading or listening to this book and for engaging in my work at bemorewithless.com. Some of you have been reading since I started writing there in 2010! We've grown so much together. Your kind messages, notes of support, and the way you share your progress and celebrations inspires me to keep writing.

Thank you to the lovely people in my membership program. You've been receiving my gentle messages for years and seeing you support each other and become more gentle in your own lives let me see how important it was to get this message out in the world.

Thank you to my wonderful agent, Wendy Sherman. This is our third book together and you have been my champion, my friend, and my connection to so many brilliant people in the publishing world. I'm so grateful for the relationships you've cultivated and shared with me.

Richelle Fredson, I've written two other books but until I met you, I didn't really know how to write a powerful book proposal. Working with you changed the way *Gentle* was received and I'm so grateful for our work together.

I have so much gratitude for the women I've worked with as part of the Be More with Less team: Melissa Thorpe, Tammy Strobel, Gina Colon, and Sophie Harding, you've helped me grow in so many ways. Thank you.

For my editors...Hannah Robinson, thank you for believing in my work, seeing my vision for *Gentle*, and bringing me to Grand Central Publishing's Balance. Marsha Shandur, thank you for your brilliant recommendations and for making me smile so much with your "Put it on a T-Shirt!" comments on the parts you loved. Sara Carder, I was over the moon when I learned we'd be working together again. I love what you bring to my writing. You get me. I love you.

Nana Twumasi, Natalie Bautista, and the team at Balance, thank you for all your support in turning my gentle idea into this beautiful book.

I'm so grateful for my friends and family who cheered me on as I wrote this book. I love you.

Thank you to Mark for never complaining and always supporting me as I took extra time away to write this book, for quitting social media, and for watching my favorite movies even though they aren't always his. Now that I think about it, it has been a while since we watched *The Holiday*. I love you.

Alyson, you are one of my absolute favorite people. I love our daily chats, coffee time, laughing until we cry, traveling the world, reminding each other of all the things we forget, and supporting each other in a way that only sisters can. I love you.

Bailey, I started and ended this book with you because you mean everything to me. I love you so much.

Notes

PART I: REST

1. Kevin Dickinson, "The World Must Learn from 'Karoshi,' Japan's Overwork Epidemic—Before It's Too Late," *Big Think* (blog), January 24, 2023, accessed April 10, 2024, https://bigthink.com/the-learning-curve/karoshi/.

2. Nicola Jane Hobbs (@nicolajanehobbs), "Instead of asking, 'Have I worked hard enough to deserve to rest?', I've started asking, 'Have I rested enough to do my most loving, meaningful work?',' Instagram, January 5, 2023, https://www.instagram.com/p/CnCrIrntY7_/?hl=en&img_index=1.

3. Lewis Howes and Dr. Matthew Walker, in "Dr. Matthew Walker: Why We Should Prioritize Sleep & Understanding the Impact of Dreams (Part 1)," *The School of Greatness*, episode 1154, podcast, MP3 audio, 01:01:09, https://lewishowes.com/podcast/why-we-should-prioritize-sleep-understanding-the-impact-of-dreams-with-dr-matthew-walker/.

4. Tricia Hersey, *Rest Is Resistance: A Manifesto* (London: Little, Brown Spark, 2022).

5. Tricia Hersey, The Nap Ministry, accessed December 8, 2023, https://thenapministry.com/.

6. Leah Smith, "#Ableism," Center for Disability Rights, accessed December 13, 2023, https://cdrnys.org/blog/uncategorized/ableism/.

ONE: Rest First

1. Brené Brown, "Clear Is Kind. Unclear Is Unkind.," Brené Brown (website), last modified October 15, 2018, https://brenebrown.com/articles/2018/10/15/clear-is-kind-unclear-is-unkind/.

TWO: Little Saturday

1. Leo Babauta, "Tea Rituals for Focus, Health & Slowness," *Zen Habits* (blog), accessed December 8, 2023, https://zenhabits.net/tea-rituals/.
2. Marisa Mayes (@itsmarisajo), "#BareMinimumMonday—the part of me that's dying to be set free from hustle culture," TikTok, video, May 23, 2022, https://www.tiktok.com/@itsmarisajo/video/7101123330563968299?lang=en.
3. Karlee Flores (@karleesislerflores), Instagram, accessed December 8, 2023, https://www.instagram.com/karleesislerflores/.

FOUR: Underreact

1. Melissa Urban, *The Book of Boundaries* (New York: Random House, 2023).
2. Melissa Urban (@melissau), "Brush up today to make sure your holiday boundaries are successful," Instagram Reel, November 22, 2023, https://www.instagram.com/p/Cz9IGW_xQd4/.

FIVE: Be Green–Adjacent

1. Courtney Carver and Bailey Carver, "45. Plants Make People Happy: Interview with Eliza Blank, Founder and CEO of The Sill," *Soul & Wit*, October 19, 2020, podcast, MP3 audio, 36:14, https://podcasts.apple.com/us/podcast/soul-and-wit/id1489742667?i=1000495252860.
2. "The Benefits of Houseplants," *The Sill* (blog), accessed December 11, 2023, https://www.thesill.com/pages/mood-boosting-house plants.
3. Lala Tanmoy Das, "What Science Tells Us About the Mood-Boosting Effects of Indoor Plants," *Washington Post*, June 7, 2022, https://www.washingtonpost.com/wellness/2022/06/06/how-houseplants-can-boost-your-mood/.
4. Marlon Nieuwenhuis, Craig Knight, Tom Postmes, and S. Alexander Haslam, "The Relative Benefits Of Green Versus Lean Office Space: Three Field Experiments," *Journal of Experimental Psychology: Applied* 20, no. 3 (2014), https://pubmed.ncbi.nlm.nih.gov/25068481/.

SIX: Break Up with Breaking News

1. Michael Easter, *Scarcity Brain: Fix Your Craving Mindset and Rewire Your Habits to Thrive with Enough* (New York: Rodale Books, 2023).

2. Byron Katie, "Staying in Your Own Business," *Awakin.org* (blog), accessed December 11, 2023, https://www.awakin.org/v2/read/view.php?tid=997.
3. Sharon McMahon (@sharonsaysso), "The antidote to despair is action. When you feel overwhelmed by bad news, instead of thinking about it nonstop like a hamster on a wheel or choosing to ignore it because you can't see a way to fix it and you're only one person, do something small and imperfect.", Instagram, November 29, 2023, https://www.instagram.com/p/C0PElSAuhLC/.

SEVEN: Go to Bed

1. Maria Godoy and Audrey Nguyen, "Stop Doomscrolling and Get Ready for Bed. Here's How to Reclaim a Good Night's Sleep," *Life Kit*, NPR, June 16, 2022, https://www.npr.org/2022/06/14/1105122521/stop-revenge-bedtime-procrastination-get-better-sleep.

EIGHT: Find Connection

1. Rachel Shanken, "Are You Having Fun Yet?" *MindBodyWise* (blog), https://mindbodywise.com/blog/are-you-having-fun-yet/.
2. "Somatic Therapy," *Psychology Today*, accessed December 11, 2023, https://www.psychologytoday.com/us/therapy-types/somatic-therapy.
3. Iris Goldsztajn, "What Is Somatic Therapy?," *The Good Trade* (blog), May 30, 2023, https://www.thegoodtrade.com/features/what-is-somatic-therapy/.
4. Pooja Agarwal, Zahra Sebghatollahi, Mehnaz Kamal, et al., "Citrus Essential Oils in Aromatherapy: Therapeutic Effects and Mechanisms," *Antioxidants (Basel)* 11, no. 12 (December 2022), https://www.ncbi.nlm.nih.gov/pmc/articles/PMC9774566/.

PART II: LESS

1. Chris Weller, "A Neuroscientist Explains Why He Always Picks the 2nd Menu Item on a List of Specials," *Business Insider*, July 28, 2017, https://www.businessinsider.com/neuroscientist-decision-making-hack-restaurants-2017-7.

ONE: Home Release

1. Courtney Carver, "Project 333," Be More with Less, https://bemorewithless.com/project-333/.

THREE: Count Your Spoons

1. "Spoon Theory," Wikipedia, accessed December 14, 2023, https://en.wikipedia.org/wiki/Spoon_theory. https://www.healthline.com/health/spoon-theory-chronic-illness-explained-like-never-before#2.
2. Kylie Logan, "A CEO Who Implemented a 4-Day Workweek in July Says Her Company 'Will Never Go Back.' It Boosted Revenue and Morale," *Fortune*, December 1, 2021, https://fortune.com/2021/12/01/ceo-4-day-work-week/amp/.

SIX: Unplug

1. Tiffany Shlain, *24/6: Giving Up Screens One Day a Week to Get More Time, Creativity and Connection* (New York: Gallery Books, 2020).
2. Jack Flynn, "20 Vital Smartphone Usage Statistics [2023]: Facts, Data, and Trends on Mobile Use in the U.S.," Zippia: The Career Expert, April 3, 2023, https://www.zippia.com/advice/smartphone-usage-statistics/.

SEVEN: Drink Less

1. Amelia Nierenberg, "Why Does Alcohol Mess with My Sleep?," *New York Times*, January 25, 2022, https://www.nytimes.com/2022/01/25/well/mind/alcohol-drinking-sleep.html.
2. "Sleep," *New York Times*, accessed December 14, 2023, https://www.nytimes.com/2022/01/25/well/mind/alcohol-drinking-sleep.html.
3. Aaron M. White, "What Happened? Alcohol, Memory Blackouts, and the Brain," *Alcohol Research & Health* 27, no. 2 (2003): 186–196, https://www.ncbi.nlm.nih.gov/pmc/articles/PMC6668891/.
4. Laura McKowen, *We Are the Luckiest: The Surprising Magic of a Sober Life* (Novato, CA: New World Library, 2020).

NINE: Less Organizing

1. "Global Home Organization Products Market Report 2023–2030: Continuing Trend of Working from Home Bolsters Growth," *Yahoo! Finance,* May 10, 2023, https://finance.yahoo.com/news/global-home-organization-products-market-100800006.html.
2. Myquillyn Smith, "31 Days : Nobody's Dream Job," *Nesting Place* (blog), October 8, 2012, https://thenester.com/2012/10/31-days-nobodys-dream-job.html.

3. Ashley Abramson, "Use Temptation Bundling to Create Better Habits," *Forge*, June 21, 2019, Medium, https://forge.medium.com /use-temptation-bundling-to-create-better-habits-46ada663fb1d.

4. Katherine L. Milkman, Julia A. Minson, and Kevin G. M. Volpp, "Holding the Hunger Games Hostage at the Gym: An Evaluation of Temptation Bundling," *Management Science* 60, no. 2 (2014): 283–299, https://www.ncbi.nlm.nih.gov/pmc/articles/PMC4381662/.

ELEVEN: Less Regret

1. Elise Hu and Andee Tagle, "How Examining Our Regrets Can Make for a More Meaningful Life," *Life Kit*, NPR, December 21, 2022, https://www.npr.org/2022/03/16/1087010308/the-power-of-regret -how-examining-regret-can-help-you-live-a-meaningful-life.

PART III: RISE

TWO: Be Gentle Anytime

1. Elizabeth Gilbert and Brené Brown, "Magic Lessons Se. 1, Ep. 12: Brené Brown on 'Big Strong Magic,'" *Magic Lessons with Elizabeth Gilbert*, July 25, 2016, podcast, MP3 audio, 35:22, https://podcasts .apple.com/us/podcast/magic-lessons-with-elizabeth-gilbert /id1138081319?i=1000373139417.

2. Rosamund Stone Zander and Benjamin Zander, *The Art of Possibility: Transforming Professional and Personal Life* (New York: Penguin Books, 2002).

THREE: Don't Take It Personally

1. Elyse Myers, "I Don't Receive That," YouTube, March 7, 2022, video, 0:51, https://www.youtube.com/watch?v=jSXkO5ehoOU.

2. Glennon Doyle, *Untamed* (New York: The Dial Press, 2020).

FOUR: Go Slowly

1. Sierra is probably reading (@sierranwells), "My therapist said: 'remember that the other side of giving your all is being empty. And if you continue to give your all, you'll continue to be empty. Giving your all is unregulated and has no boundaries. Give your best.' WHEW," X (formerly known as Twitter), February 14, 2022, https://x.com/sierranwells/status/1493413863143976960/.

FIVE: Cultivate Quiet

1. Thich Nhat Hanh, "Walk Like a Buddha," *Tricycle*, Summer 2011, https://tricycle.org/magazine/walk-buddha/.

EIGHT: Ask Yourself

1. Peter Sowell (@Motherly), "Viral video of little girl wearing lipstick from 'Home Depot,'" Facebook, video, September 23, 2019, https://www.facebook.com/watch/?v=688114118335472.
2. Noëlle de Leeuw, "Are You Lonely? Join These Women for a Walk in the Park," *Elle*, May 25, 2023, https://www.elle.com/life-love/a43990707/city-girls-who-walk-new-york-city/.

Index